The Death of Granny Doe

A slippery slope

Terence Morrissey

Bloomington, IN  Milton Keynes, UK

AuthorHouse™
1663 Liberty Drive, Suite 200
Bloomington, IN 47403
www.authorhouse.com
Phone: 1-800-839-8640

AuthorHouse™ UK Ltd.
500 Avebury Boulevard
Central Milton Keynes, MK9 2BE
www.authorhouse.co.uk
Phone: 08001974150

© 2006 Terence Morrissey. All rights reserved.

No part of this book may be reproduced, stored in a retrieval system, or transmitted by any means without the written permission of the author.

First published by AuthorHouse 4/10/2006

ISBN: 1-4259-2338-0 (sc)

Library of Congress Control Number: 2006902333

Printed in the United States of America
Bloomington, Indiana

This book is printed on acid-free paper.

This book is dedicated to my Grandmother,
Who is but a vague but beautiful memory.

CONTENTS

Acknowledgements And Disclaimer ix

Chapter One
The Question 1

Chapter Two
The Right To Life 9

Chapter Three
An Obligation To Die 15

Chapter Four
Worth Value And Dignity 23

Chapter Five
After The Slaughter, Is Rachel Still Weeping? 27

Chapter Six
The Veterans Of Abortion 31

Chapter Seven
Dislocation Of Purpose 37

Chapter Eight
The Subordinate Female 41

Chapter Nine
Acquiescent Yet Angry 45

Chapter Ten
The Vanishing Male 49

Chapter Eleven
Alienation From Parents 53

Chapter Twelve
Resentment Of Those Closest 57

Chapter Thirteen
Women And Men Set At Odds 61

Chapter Fourteen
A Choice Of Muddled Choosing 67

Chapter Fifteen
Hostility To Father, Hostility To Child 73

Chapter Sixteen
Women Disengaged 77

Chapter Seventeen
Reasons For Not Wanting A Child 79

Chapter Eighteen
A Matter Of Necessity 87

Chapter Nineteen
Adoption As An Alternative 91

Chapter Twenty
Is There A Child At Stake? 99

Chapter Twenty One
Incoherent Reasons, Incoherent Misgivings ... 105

Chapter Twenty Two
Reluctance About Moral Judgment 113

Chapter Twenty Three
Who Are The Abortors 119

Chapter Twenty Four
A Fundamental Right* 125

Roe V Wade
Writing The Final Chapter 127

The Author's Personal Letter To A Friend 129

*biographical Notes: Father James Burtchaell: 135

ACKNOWLEDGEMENTS AND DISCLAIMER

Gratitude, a word worn thin by usage, nonetheless continues to convey to the recipient the sincerest "Thank You" that the beneficiary can possibly extend. It is with this thought in mind that I offer to Deenie Lusse, my sincerest gratitude for her true friendship and for being a very able friend and also for her time and expertise in editing this booklet.

I would be remiss if I neglected to thank Father James Burtchaell, not only for allowing me the honor of copying a huge segment of the first Essay of his book 'Rachel Weeping,' but also for his kindness in offering to proof read this manuscript.

My son, Michael contributed many hours of his and his graphic company's time to produce a magnificent eye catching cover. To you 'Mike' heartfelt thanks for your love and support.

I wish to point out that there are those that have assisted me in many ways in the compiling of this booklet. Their contributions do not in any way imply that they are in agreement with the subject matter.

Deenie Lusse who edited the manuscript and my son Michael who contributed time and effort to the graphics of the front cover and the picture on the back cover do not hold to these views. But I am grateful for their love and their willing spirit to assist me.

The Cover:

As I have mentioned above, the cover graphics were contributed by absolute_graphics @hotmail.com a company owned and operated by Michael Morrissey. As an interesting aside the knife that is depicted as stabbing the heart is the actual knife that Booth was carrying when he assassinated Abraham Lincoln.

Terence Morrissey

CHAPTER ONE
THE QUESTION

Can a man (or woman) be held responsible for murder or killing if he or she did not actually pull the trigger of a gun, or plunge the knife, or by any means cause another person to no longer live?

History records that "Hitler killed 12 million people." But as far as can be determined he did not actually kill anyone himself, he caused them to be killed.

History further records that Stalin killed 18 million people. But, again, it is recorded that he did not actually kill those people himself. He was the cause of their deaths by virtue of his office and/or position.

If the answer to the above question, in the first paragraph, is yes, then it is safe to say that Hitler and Stalin are as guilty as the ones who actually committed the murders (even under the guise of performed wartime activities). Has not the highest court, of any country also caused the deaths of untold millions of human beings by its decision to allow abortion on demand? And in many cases encouraged it?

Consider the following….

Karl Marx insisted that "In our evolutionary conception of the universe, there is absolutely no room for either a creator or a ruler."

Hitler justified his actions, in the extermination of millions of men, women and children (including the unborn), on the basis of evolution, declaring in his book MEIN KAMPF" (1924) that "If nature does not wish that the weaker individuals should mate with the stronger, then she (nature) wishes even less that a superior race like the Germanic race should intermingle with an inferior one. Why? Because in such a case her (nature's) efforts, throughout hundreds of thousands of years, to establish an evolutionary higher stage of being, may thus be rendered futile."

In 1859, Charles Darwin wrote "On the Origin of Species" followed by "The Descent of Man" (1871). In these two books he concluded that mankind had evolved from lower forms of life. And so with this single argument (evolution) the complete mystery of the universe is not only explained, but also solved. A creator is annulled and all the knowledge that ever there was, up to this statement (concerning creation) was relegated to the trash heap of insanity and henceforth considered non-knowledge

This leaves us with the timely question, "What is Darwinism?" In a word it is "Atheism." Darwinism can, without hesitation be described as "Atheism." The fact that Mr. Darwin excludes any design from nature precludes the fact that there is no designer. Further, if Darwin (evolution) says there was (is) no creation he then, flippantly, leaves us with the very simple conclusion that there was (is) no creator.

I might point out that evolution is still mandated just a "Theory." I might further point out that one person's theory is as valid as the next person's. At this juncture it would not be unkind to Mr. Darwin to say that the theory of any one of us (regarding how we all came to be here) would have as much validity as evolution, even if our theory was diametrically opposed to evolution.

Therefore your theory, of how man came to be, is every bit as valid as Darwin's theory. Never and I repeat, never has the word "Fact" been associated with Darwinism or evolution. "FACT" IS PROVEN BEYOND A SHADOW OF A DOUBT, AN OUTCOME DETERMINED BY ABSOLUTE EVIDENCE AND OBJECTIVELY VERIFIED, whereby Darwin's theory, of how mankind came to be, is just a good guess based on unverified research, lacking proof or substantiation.

The Russian novelist Dostoevsky has noted in his book "The Brothers Karamazov," that if God did not exist, then everything is lawful. Following this line of thinking, that humans were not created, but rather evolved from lower animals, it is easy to conclude how and why both Hitler and Stalin justified their ghastly slaughter of millions of human beings.

When all the arguments for the mass destruction of human life are reduced to the bottom line, using the rationale of Hitler, Darwin, Stalin, et al, they amount to this; "Man is an animal and as such, all undesired animals can be weeded out of the human herd."

Nobel Prize winning professor J. Watson (for example) recommended that in order to avoid "Birth defects," no child should be declared alive until three days after birth.

In testimony before a presidential commission, philosopher Mary Ann Warren compared a disabled newborn child with a horse that had to be killed because it had a broken leg.

Peter Singer insists that "The life of a newborn baby is of less value than the life of a pig, a dog, or chimpanzee". He even went so far as to say that his conclusions "apply to the newborn baby as much as to the fetus."

Now let us move on. We might look at the fact that abortion has, without a shadow of a doubt, led to infanticide, as noted in the American Heritage Dictionary "The killing of an infant, a child killer."

Everything must have a beginning and abortion is only the start of worse things to come and in fact are already here. It should be quite obvious that killing tiny human beings before they are born is leading, as stated above, to the killing of them after they are born.

This is already occurring. One of the approved methods of abortion is Hysterotomy or more commonly known as a C-section. In this method the baby is aborted alive and must then be killed by cutting off oxygen, by drowning, or by starvation. Occasionally a metal instrument through the heart does the job quite nicely.

A professor of pediatrics at the University of Wisconsin stated sadly, "It is common in the United States of America to withhold routine surgery and medical care, for infants with Downs's syndrome, for the explicit purpose of hastening death." (Archives of internal medicine, Dec. 1982).

Dr. Peter A.J. Adams, of Case Western Reserve University, cut off the heads of 12 tiny babies born alive by hysterotomy

©-section) abortion. He then pumped blood into their brains to keep them alive, much the way Russians did with heads of dogs in the 1950's.

In responding to an outcry over his experiments, Dr. Adams declared, "Once society) The Supreme Court) declared the fetus dead and abrogated) took away its (the baby's) rights, I don't see any ethical problem...Whose rights are we going to protect, once we've decided the fetus won't live?"

Indeed, abortion has been used to justify widespread fetal experimentation. For example, in 1973 kidneys were taken from aborted babies for study at Dalhousie University in Canada. The New England Journal of Medicine (vol.28, no. 23) reported on a study of the effects of a mother's drugs on her babies that were aborted alive.

According to the American Journal of Obstetrics and Gynecology (Jan. 1974), Dr. Bela A. Resch cut hearts out of aborted babies. The hearts kept beating for hours. In another case a doctor, at a University in Canada, cut open the skulls of live babies and studied them. He later killed the babies by a sharp puncture to the heart.

Dr. Martin Kekomaki cut open the stomachs and cut off the heads of live aborted babies in 1980 and in 2003 the news reported that brain tissue is being taken from live aborted babies for a transplant into patients with Parkinson's disease.

The medical profession, the legal profession, groups who favor abortion including the highest courts of two of the supposed 'most' enlightened countries have tried to convince us that abortion is "OK" because it (the fetus) is not alive. Well we might respond, "Whoever heard of using dead tissue in transplants?"

CONTRARY to the wishes of the MAJORITY of its citizens, many a Supreme Court has ruled that the unborn are not human persons protected by their (country's) constitution.

I can't help but wonder how those sitting on those same courts would feel if a law was passed declaring that all the children, of those sitting on any higher court, were "not human persons protected by any constitution." After all is said and done, the bottom line is this, 'each one of us is a fetus that grew up to become an adult.'

In the wake of the decision by the Supreme Court and what one dissenting justice called "an act of raw judicial power," more than 150 million unborn children (as of this writing) have been robbed of their right to life.

One of the most amazing aspects of this decision is the fact that the highest courts knew that if they agreed that the fetus was a person then the unborn child would have been protected by the (fourteenth) amendment. Here is how they worded this thought. "If this suggestion of personhood is established, the appellant's case of course collapses, for the fetus' right to life is then guaranteed specifically by the (fourteenth) amendment."

Part of the argument for abortion is that "The woman has a right to do what she wants with her body." If you buy into this argument then it is obvious that you should be defending the 'Right' of a woman to stand on a street corner and stick a needle in her arm and shoot poison into her veins, after all haven't some of you said that a woman's body is her own to do with as she wants...or does this so called ridiculous argument only apply to killing the unborn? Or to exaggerate the illustration (with some semblance of actuality based on the right of a woman to do what she wants with her own body). If a woman doused herself with gasoline and set herself on fire, then the authorities and the fire department would be required to stand by as she burned to death (which we know is absolutely ludicrous in the extreme) because she is doing what she wants with her new found freedom to deal with her body as she wishes.

Not only has the right to life been taken away from unborn humans by the courts, but apparently so has the right to be buried as such. In 1983 some 16,000 aborted babies were found in a storage container in California.

A Civil Liberties group protested the plans of some "Pro-Lifers" to bury the babies. Let me tell you on what these supposedly "Enlightened" individuals based their argument.

They (The Civil Liberties Group) insisted that the court had ruled that the unborn are not human and, hence, should not be buried like humans.

Ironically, the Civil Liberties Group made no protests against the burial of cats and dogs in animal cemeteries. It is no exaggeration to say that in some countries today animals are treated like humans and humans are treated like animals. In the not too distant past "Man used to love people and use things, today he loves things and uses people."

On May 14th, 1984, the Milwaukee Sentinel reported that police arrested four children, ages four to 11, who were throwing a fetus off a bridge. The youngsters had retrieved 22 aborted babies from a nearby dumpster. When asked what they were doing, the children replied that they were playing with "little people."

I can't help but speculate on the fact that the higher court, the medical profession, the members of the Civil Liberties Group and the "Pro Choice" screamers were not as alert as these youngsters and notice that the decision they were making involved "little people."One further wonders why the members of the above groups did not know what the "unpolluted minds" of these children knew.

It should not amaze any of us that the children were treating the babies like garbage. That is exactly where the "grown ups" had thrown them.

In an attempt to justify his experiments on live babies, Dr. Matti Kekomaki said bluntly, "an aborted baby is just garbage and that's where it ends up" (National Examiner, August 19, 1980).

CHAPTER TWO
THE RIGHT TO LIFE

In America, the Fourteenth Amendment guarantees "the right to life....." for all Americans. And this "right to life" should extend to unborn humans. Thomas Jefferson spoke of human right to life as an "unalienable" right given by the creator. But what was given by the creator has been taken away by the Supreme Court. In Canada there is a similar guarantee in the "Charter of Rights."

Before a congressional hearing in April of 1981, the noted geneticist, Dr. Hymie Gordan testified, "It is an established scientific fact...that all life, including human life, begins at conception."

The world famous geneticist Jerome Jejune declared, "The fact that after fertilization has taken place a new human has come into being is no longer a matter of (individual) 'taste' or opinion."

When does human life begin? It begins at conception (fertilization). Both scripture and science agree with this conclusion. David, of the bible, said, "In sin did my mother conceive me." The angel said of Mary, "What is conceived in her is from the Holy Spirit." The psalmist describes the embryo as a "Wonderful creation of God, known personally by God and even written in HIS book."

The most crucial passage on the topic is to be found in Exodus and is translated by the great Hebrew scholar, U. Cassuto, as follows: When men strive together and they hurt unintentionally a woman with a child and her children come forth and no mischief happens - that is, the woman and the child do not die - the one who hurts her shall be punished by a fine. But if any mischief happens, that is, if the woman dies, or the children, then you shall give life for life.

This "life for life" penalty for killing the unborn leave no doubt that God considered the life of the unborn to be of equal value to that of the mother.

Why is human life valued so highly? It is because God created man in HIS image and likeness. And the image of God includes "male and female". It is a scientific fact that sex is determined at the moment of conception, thus making it clear that the image of God in a new life begins at the very moment of conception.

At the hub of Christian/Judeo moral theology is the belief that life is sacred, is given by God and is to be taken only through means designated by him. One of the major assaults on this teaching has been the onslaught of abortion in the last two decades in various nations around the world.

When this departure from American/Canadian-Christian/Judeo ethics began, many argued that the next step would be euthanasia. Tragically, these predications have proved true. Today it seems that the 'right to die' has replaced the 'right to life' concept and is being accepted by a large number of people in our culture.

But do we really have a "right" to die? May we decide at any given moment that we can take the life of the elderly, the infirm, the mentally disabled or the lives of our unborn children?

If you will bear with me, I will attempt to show you just where abortion leads. In the next few paragraphs we will see that abortion and euthanasia are pretty well yoked together.

In fact it might be said that they are walking hand-in-hand down death's road and have met up with their companion, "infanticide."

Highly respected scientists (as already noted) are openly recommending infanticide for genetic reasons. The Nazis began the same way. What is frightening is the extent to which this may be taken.

Professor Michael Tooley of Stanford University argues that one is not a person unless he is "self conscious." But children do not become "self-conscious" until they are about a year and a half old. Based on this conclusion there appears to be justification to kill a child well into his or her second year!

In the September 6, 1982 issue of Newsweek Magazine, a headline in the article read, "Biologists say infanticide is as normal as the sex drive - and that most animals, including man, practice it." Next to the headline was a picture of a mother baboon killing her baby. The implication of the article was that if baboons are doing it, why shouldn't we?

Since when did animals become the standard for human behavior? It is ironic to note that even animals do not kill their offspring in the percentages that humans do. Statistics show that one out of every three pregnancies is terminated by abortion.

In some places, another means of termination is being used; On June 21, 1986, the Associated Press reported that doctors in the Netherlands used "Selective termination" on a woman carrying quintuplets. They killed three and she gave birth to only two babies. It was reported that the mother took the step because she "was disturbed over the prospects of having quintuplets."

So now we are playing "Follow the leader" but unfortunately where the leader is taking us may not be exactly where we want to go and very soon we just might be in too deep to turn back. Similarly, as abortion leads to euthanasia (the killing of anything, human or animal regardless of age), then euthanasia leads to infanticide (the killing of a baby well after it is born).

You can readily see that size and age make absolutely no difference once people can be declared "Nonhuman." In 1973, the Human Manifesto II declared that suicide and euthanasia are entirely acceptable.

Politicians are even getting into the act openly, whereas in the past they succumbed to that rhetoric that guaranteed votes but avoided any direct reference to life and death issues that made it appear that they were taking a stance.

On occasion when they did make a stand and it looked like the "Voting" tide was turning against them, they found, for the sake of expediency, it was necessary to change horses in midstream. And change horses they did, something that happens (unfortunately) all too often in various spectrums.

Being for life does not necessarily qualify a candidate for public office. However being against life (i.e.: murdering your grandmother (Euthanasia), killing your disabled baby (Infanticide), or forcing you to abort your child for the "welfare" of the population), should automatically disqualify ANY PERSON from holding public office.

It does not suffice to say "I am personally opposed to abortion, but I do not object if others have them." No one in his or her right mind would apply this kind of logic to child abuse, rape or murder.

The logical connection between abortion, infanticide and euthanasia is very strong. They involve the same patient, the same procedure, the same rationale and sadly, the same result. As the late Princeton ethicist Paul Ramsey observed, "There are many good reasons for abortion but unfortunately these same reasons also (can be used) to justify infanticide and euthanasia."

We can and should, USE OUR VOTE to take a stand against this senseless slaughter of the disabled, the elderly and the unborn.

CHAPTER THREE
AN OBLIGATION TO DIE

As we continue to explore this life and death issue we will examine what has brought us to this intricate ethical, moral, economic and political problem with the emphasis on moral and ethical. We will see how the right to die (an outgrowth of the abortion issue), has become the right to take another person's life and how ultimately, became an obligation to die.

I will use the bible as a valuable source. I gathered much crucial information as I read through this book concerning the subject matter. The quotations below are not intended to 'Sell Christianity' or to convert anyone. I just happen to see some very enlightened parallels that I feel might assist us to make an informed decision.

According to the bible, life should be viewed as precious. Jesus wept when Lazarus died.

Innocent human life must be protected and preserved. Even life that is "Less meaningful" (and who decides when someone else's life is more or less meaningful?) than our own deserves protecting. When we protect "their" life we are ultimately protecting "our" life at some future date.

There are three types of euthanasia that I would like you to look at with me. When we use the term "euthanasia" we are in fact using a substitute word for "Kill," "To put to death," "To deprive of life." It is not, as some would have us believe, a method whereby a life is taken as an act of mercy. Euthanasia is <u>strictly</u> another word for killing or murder.

The first type of euthanasia is "Passive" euthanasia. In this form a person is simply allowed to die naturally. No special means are provided to sustain life. No attempt is made to continue bodily functions of a terminally ill patient when the end result would have no satisfactory results.

To further illustrate the above, the body is being kept alive by machines and there is no sign of life in the brain. The heart, blood circulation and breathing are all a result of a machine. I think it would be safe to say, under these circumstances, that death has already occurred. And if death has occurred, then in essence, we are sustaining bodily functions contrary to the natural laws of God.

This should not be considered "The taking of a life" and is certainly not mercy killing by any stretch of the imagination. This might be better termed the coming together of nature and in some cases, includes the plan of God. No one lives forever. I doubt if there is a requirement for man to sustain life under these circumstances.

On the other hand, when human life can be maintained with techniques that sustain the respiratory system, a functioning brain and it can be determined that these acts are simple rather than extraordinary and would prolong life in the face of imminent death, then human kindness and respect for human life dictates use of these means.

Euthanasia (in the sense we are discussing) is 'Active.' It is little different from the act of pulling the trigger of a gun, strangulation or the plunging of a sharp instrument into someone's heart.

All of these methods, of killing, like euthanasia, take premeditation and exertion. Not one person can stand in front of another person, wish they would die and have it come to pass. Someone must be actively involved in administering euthanasia.

Dr. Davis defines it this way, "The deliberate killing of a person suffering an illness believed to be terminal, seemingly out of mercy is (unacceptable and inexcusable)." In most cases, it is done for selfish motives.

These motives might include economic motives: Doctors' bills, hospital bills, cost of a care centre, etc...Social motives: Embarrassment, curtailing of family activities, interfering with business advantages, etc.

Moral motives: Judgment of right or wrong, exhibiting a standard of what is right and just, performing a moral obligation, setting a standard, etc. In other words setting oneself up as Judge, Jury, executioner and ultimately 'God.'

This is termed "active euthanasia," and may be voluntary or involuntary for the patient.

Voluntary euthanasia generally falls into the category of the following: Some, who are under the impression that their life is not worth living or that death is preferable to sickness or pain, may ask someone to take their life-or they may take it themselves.

Euthanasia sometimes occurs when one partner in a long marriage takes the life of the other because he or she cannot stand to see their loved one suffer.

Periodically, newspaper reports tell of nurses or medical doctors who administer lethal drugs to kill their patients, supposedly out of "Compassion." But either type of active euthanasia is reprehensible and contrary to the basic natural law of man and his instinctive ethical values.

As Thomas Wood has said, "The right to life is God given and it is not within the moral competence of man, deliberately and directly, to take the life of any innocent human being either with or without his (or her) consent...a man is not the absolute owner of his life. It belongs to the life giver, God. Man has the right (and obligation) to prolong it and preserve it but he does not have the right, (and certainly not the obligation), to destroy it.

It's a frightening thing that Hitler had taken his country and its people to the exact same spot that a host of other countries are heading in today, regarding life and death decisions of other humans.

My dear friends don't stop now. Read on and let me share something with you that you might find astonishing.

It would surprise most people to find that the "Death Ovens" and the wholesale slaughter of human beings under that "Nightmare Regime" in Germany were not originally intended for the Jewish people.

The first victims were the aged, physically disabled and the mentally incompetent. The medical community of Germany was primarily responsible for the horror that descended in its full fury with Adolph Hitler.

Hitler simply took advantage of and enhanced the same "philosophy" already held by some doctors in that society and is becoming prevalent in other societies, which is... "No special moral conscience came with a MD degree in prewar Germany."

Sadly, there are some in the medical profession and in the legal profession, today, who are lacking any moral conscience. Let it be understood that in most professions the majority of those professionals are good, decent, honorable and ethical men and women. Unfortunately the minority seem to be able to gather unto themselves those in powerful positions that would assist them in furthering their own personal agendas. Abortion and euthanasia being at the top of the list.

Before abortion, infanticide, euthanasia or any other crime against humanity can receive public approval, it must first have "professional" approval, legal, medical and then government. We have a tendency (mistakenly so) to hold some of these professions up on a godlike pedestal. When in reality there are those in these professions, who have gathered power unto themselves and who are forcing their moral and ethical standards (or lack of them) on a greater percentage of the people than care to have them.

In Holland, the right-to-kill legislation was approved in 1981. The Dutch courts stipulated four conditions: unbearable pain (ever heard of pain killers?) patient consciousness, patient consent and witnesses to consent. Ten years later, the Dutch government's Remmelink Report found that almost 10% of

Dutch deaths are now being inflicted by doctors, of which 60% occur without permission of the patient and in almost half those cases without the family knowing. Doctors simply falsify death certificates. Their most common excuse for murdering patients is "Low Quality of life." Dutch specialists offer self help courses to suicidal teens. People with serious medical problems carry cards asking "Not to be killed" if they are admitted to hospital. (British Columbia Report March 14, 1994).

Let me once again point out that, in any profession, there are those that operate under very high moral and ethical standards just as the majority of the public also operate under these same high moral and ethical standards.

Nonetheless, a "Concept of God" must be adopted by those in power before public approval is obtained to carry out crimes against humanity. If God's laws can be weakened or appear to be of little or no consequence concerning life and death and this "Concept" is approved by those in power (as in Hitler's Germany) then public approval is all but guaranteed.

There are several "Conceptions of God" and which view society holds - at least in the power enforcing aspects of society - will ultimately make all the difference. For example, if your religion, church, etc. has taken a backward step concerning God's view on life and death, then there is an excellent chance you will also.

The theory of evolution has caused many to believe that man is simply an evolved animal and therefore must be judged as an animal. This, unfortunately, leaves us without any moral basis on which to base decisions, since animal activities are amoral (which defines as "lacking any moral sensibility, making no moral distinction, or caring what is right or wrong").

Others see man as merely an economic being (the theology of economics) having good worth only as long as he or she contributes to the good of the State. This socialistic perspective sees the advancement of the state as the goal of all individuals. Therefore, the individual, you and I, your unborn baby, the malformed or the elderly may be sacrificed for the good of the people.

The last, most recent and relatively popular (but by no means majority) view is that of man as a machine, we are valuable only as long as we are functioning properly, in good shape and contributing significantly to the welfare and well-being of those in power.

Man is to be subservient and should view himself as a cog in the larger picture of the human machine. When better parts (humans) become available, then the lesser, inferior or broken parts (humans) are simply discarded by way of death.

These views and accomplishments pervade our society today - though under different and various names - and they form the not-so-secret foundation for the increasing widespread death (euthanasia) of countless helpless human beings in the world today. And are in stark contrast to the beliefs of the forefathers and founding fathers of this nation that they found in the bible.

CHAPTER FOUR
WORTH VALUE AND DIGNITY

The bible presents the worth, value and dignity of man as the direct result of being created in the image of God.

So where do we get the value, worth and dignity of man, by whose measuring sticks do we judge these things? Please read on while I share something of significance with you.

Listen to the words of God that are found in the creation account of man and woman (found in Genesis), where God created man, male and female and gave them the capacity to rule over the earth HE had made:

"God created man in HIS own image, in the image of God he created him; male and female he created them." God blessed them and said to them, "be fruitful and increase in number; fill the earth and subdue it."

Remember that God was speaking to you and me as individuals when HE speaks of "multiplying and subduing." HE does not indicate that we are to be subdued and not multiply (abortion) either collectively or individually.

It was never intended that we should give up our rights and be subdued by an immoral group of "individuals" whether they are called the "Government," "Pro Choice," "Right to die" or any other name.

Any group of individuals, exerting their lack of morals or values on the vast majority of the people whom neither wanted, requested, nor voted for them, should be denied that exercise at any cost.

A small group of power hungry individuals that would exercise absolute control over the minds and bodies of all those they can subdue is reprehensible and contrary to the concept of democracy and majority rule.

The "Image" of God came from being specifically created by God, to be "creators" in our own right by obeying His command to subdue the earth and multiply.

Certainly there are those that have abused this idea. There are Christian cults and non-Christian cults that have turned the word of God to their own use, deceiving many by taking a fraction of the truth and building a lie around it to ensnare those that are weak minded and are willing to be snared.

But these few abusers must not allow us to shrink from the truth that being made in the image of God dictates to us the twofold command to procreate and subdue (rule over) the earth.

These are creative acts and if they are used wisely, apart from the degenerate and greedy disposition of man, tremendous and wonderful things would be achieved endlessly. The absurd thoughts of some men and women that they were created for the sole purpose of subduing their fellow man or woman (for the good of the people?) has obscured this creative command given by God and more often than not has redirected it toward evil and selfish ends.

How do the professionals (legal, medical and government) go about getting vast hordes of individuals to agree to the killing of unborn infants (abortion), new born infants (infanticide) and the elderly (euthanasia)? Very subtly to be sure.

The best method whereby this is accomplished is the ever increasing method of misusing words, double-talk if you will. Doctors don't gather to take or remove fresh needed organs from a recently killed human; oh no, they are much more subtle and wiser than that. They hover over patients in need of care and with the clever use of double-talk, using such terminology as "treatment by withholding medical care," they "rescue" the organs they need.

To be sure there are many doctors like that amongst us today and even the acknowledged existence of one is allowing one too many. And the biggest tragedy is that it can be allowed to happen at all.

We can be ever thankful that there were (and are) those doctors who would rather die with the innocent than be party to the slaughter of the unborn, the infants and the elderly.

Having convinced the doctors that what he (Hitler) wanted was best for everybody concerned, he then turned his attention to the minds of the masses and they too, in overwhelming numbers, over a period of time were convinced.

As mentioned earlier, another reason for removing life-sustaining equipment is financial expense or merely the nuisance of treating helpless persons who eat food and have come to that place in their lives whereby they are non productive and have therefore become (in man's eyes) a valueless entity. Hitler called them "useless eaters." But we would never be found guilty of using such harsh words so we justify killing them by double-talk or word manipulation. When we kill them, it is "for their own good."

Abortion, Infanticide and Euthanasia is the ultimate abandonment of human dignity as God designed it and assigned it to the human race.

God never views the unborn, infants, the elderly, the infirm or the disabled as useless or without worth. Value in the unborn, or those born, is measured proportionately by the value we place on God because we are created in His image. Our value should not be measured by what we can do but rather by whom we are or will be in the sight of God.

Widows and the elderly in the early church were to be treated with care and that care was to be administered by the church with offerings being taken for that particular purpose.

The church today, in far too many cases, has abdicated its responsibility to the elderly, widows, the infirm, the hungry and the homeless by relinquishing the church's obligation, as mandated by God, to the government.

And the government loves and welcomes it because it puts more people under their direct control. More power to the government by an act of the church. Always bearing in mind that there are those churches and Godly people that toil endlessly, day and night, to bring peace, comfort food and clothing to those less fortunate...sadly, they are becoming less in number each day.

CHAPTER FIVE
AFTER THE SLAUGHTER,
IS RACHEL STILL WEEPING?

In the early part of 1991, I started to write a booklet about Abortion, Euthanasia and Infanticide. I have never known a person who had an abortion, I have never known a doctor or anyone else who performed and abortion or engaged in euthanasia or infanticide.

I have always had a very deep desire to 'get the facts.' I have heard arguments on many subjects and I have been engaged in plenty of discussions concerning these same topics. It slowly started to dawn on me, as I listened or engaged in a discussion, just how much of the argument, on both sides, was pure emotion.

It was obvious to me that most people are passionate about what they believe and will debate the subject until the sun comes up. Unfortunately very little of the discussion carried little, if any, convincing factual statements. I found little that indicated that any of those entering a discussion had done any research at all. Some quoted their favourite newspaper or their favourite radio or TV personality as the basis for their opinion. Sometimes they quote their neighbour, the milkman or someone they overheard on the subway or bus on their way to work. The line up of so called "Experts" is endless. In some cases (quite a few actually) these same people just made up factious characters whom they quoted as being expert in a certain field. The exaggerations, manipulation of some long lost story or straight out lies seemed to be acceptable as long as one was trying to convince the other that they were right.

In my quest for knowledge and to be able to quote with honesty anything that would strengthen my argument against abortion, euthanasia or infanticide I researched and I researched and then I researched again. In my quest for authoritive documentation I came across a book that would end my quest for sold facts. I was given a book titled "Rachel Weeping" by a friend who knew of my desire for facts. (This friend held a contrary opinion to mine but was very honest in our discussions concerning the topics in this book).

The author of "Rachel Weeping," James T. Burtchaell, had, in my estimation, researched the subject matter of my booklet to a point that would allow me to set down my researching tools and to conclude that I had all the facts I required to bring these subjects to the reader's attention. I would recommend, very highly and with great emphasis on the accuracy and incredible time that James T. Burtchael had devoted to his research. I am quoting the first chapter of "Rachel Weeping, with the very kind permission of Fr. Burtchaell.

I have not added, changed or otherwise done anything other than quote a section from the first chapter of "Rachel Weeping." If you have an honest desire to know the facts of the destructive power of Abortion, Euthanasia or Infanticide in the personal lives of those that engage in or are on the receptive end of one of these operations. If you want to know the truth about how all of us as a society, or individually are now and will continue in the future to pay a very high price for not heeding the call of the watchman that cried out "The enemy is before us."

CHAPTER SIX

THE VETERANS OF ABORTION

**(As excerpted from 'RACHEL WEEPING'
AUTHOR: Father James T. Burtchaell***
**(Used with permission)
*(See Biographical notes)
The author of "The Death of Granny Doe" has inserted a brief explanation after some of the words in the following chapters that are not in common usage today.

Some time ago then National Abortion Rights Action League bought the back page of the New York Times. The ad advised readers that the *"so-called pro-life people* are back at it," compelling women to bear unwanted children.

"But I am only twelve years old."

"I was raped."

"We'll have to go on relief."

"My father will kill me."

"The doctor says it will die before its two."

"My IUD failed."

"I'm 50; I thought I couldn't get pregnant."

The "COMPULSORY PREGNANCY" people 'have one answer to everything: 'YOU MUST HAVE THAT BABY WHETHER YOU LIKE IT OR NOT!'" readers who were asked to dig down in their genes-buttoned be they to the left or to the right-and who know the abortion scene had more to wince at than did the typesetter who had to hustle up all the boldfaced, caps and Italics.

The ad was, well, a misrepresentation. There are indeed girls who are twelve years old and pregnant, women who would need public aid, women and girls who have suffered rape and who want abortions. But these situations, desperate and tragic, put forward so strenuously by NARAL and other agencies that make the case for governmentally funded abortion on demand – these cases generally represent only a small fraction (in this instance, perhaps less than five percent) of the nearly 1,500,000 legally induced abortions in America each year.

Any public appeal is naturally going to put forward first its most needy cases, but the public also wants to know who the average beneficiaries will be. An appropriations committee deliberating over welfare budgets knows that there are widows out there who have to heat their apartments with their gas ovens; but they will vote no subsidy until they know how much real destitution is going to be alleviated by the cash and how much flimflam subsidized. Likewise, one outrageous rape–murder has us ready to lock up all young gang offenders for life; but anyone who touches the law had better first learn the full story about this sad traffic of juvenile criminals. Needs must be accurately depicted before sound public policy can be framed.

So with abortion. The American public lacks a reliable sense of who is actually sitting in those abortion clinic waiting rooms round the country. We are told they are mostly blacks; no, others say, there are crowds of suburban white matrons. Most are unmarried; no, there are more married. Their general opinion afterwards is that abortion, while not pleasant, was something they had to have at the time; no, most women will tell you that it was rotten and that they are bothered by some remorse. What is one to believe?

The most influential sources of statistics on U.S. abortion practice are the Alan Guttmacher Institute and the cluster of other agencies linked to Planned Parenthood. The best single source of statistics on the progress of the Vietnam War was General Westmoreland's office. Eventually some news people thought it didn't quite tell the full story and began to wander through the villages talking to the people. What one needs in the case of abortion, is an extended visit to the villages and that is available in Linda Bird Francke's book, *The Ambivalence of Abortion* (New York: Random House 1978; hereinafter cited as F.). After reading it one should pick up its natural supplement, *Pregnant by Mistake*, by Katrina Maxtone-Graham (New York: Liveright, 1973; hereafter cited as G).

Both books present interviews. Maxtone–Graham had extended conversations with seventeen women, who before abortion on demand was legal nationally but after it was permitted in New York. Francke offers about seventy-five interviews. They are briefer, but more varied: with women, men and couples; before, during and as much as fifty years after the abortion experience. Both authors are explicitly sympathetic to abortion choice and succeed in being relatively fair, inobtrusive interviewers. Francke writes in the aftermath of her own abortion, which she reflected on in a powerful "Jane Doe" piece on the op–ed page of the *New York Times* on May 14, 1976. That column remains one of the most haunting stories of the genre. She has three children by two marriages and when writing her book, who was sans spouse. Maxtone- Graham, also a New Yorker, who is married, with four children and much aware of her own experience of having been adopted and as an adult, having traced her physical mother and also found her brother.

Their own personal sagas lend intensity to the inquiry without skewing it. Their biases rise up in occasional questions, but the interviewees are quite determined to say it their own way and they do. In fact, so far do they stray from the conventional wisdom sustaining abortion choice today that Francke's book has gotten a few heavy frowns from fellow feminist *litteratae.*

What makes these two books helpful is that both authors have let the women and men unfold their personal experience of abortion in it all its confusion and hurt and courage and isolation. Their stories are rich and varied enough to sustain inquiry beyond (and sometimes athwart) what the interviewers say by way of summary. There is much more to be said on the subject than these people tell about their approximately one hundred abortions. But they do say much that we are rarely told and what they tell us is too large, two irreducible, to be compacted simply into percentages.

What Francke and Maxtone–Graham do not offer is any sympathetic reflections on what their interviewees have told them. Had they undertaken such an analysis, they would have seen emerging – from the veterans of the abortion experience – a profoundly unsettling story. Their documentation of the abortion experience is strong evidence – stronger in some sense that the indictments of antiabortionist-against the portrayal of abortion by its advocates.

The women who seek abortion are described by pro-choice advocates as either ordinary, sexually active women for whom contraception has failed or victimized women (victimized by a pathological pregnancy, or rape, or incest, or poverty, or family hostility). Childbirth for either group is an unreasonable burden, more than they should be obliged to cope with. Scholars who have studied women at risk for unwanted pregnancy have for some years disputed that portrayal. The stories studied here, stories recounted by abortion veterans themselves; describe a situation so different, so much more complex, that one comes to regard the pro-abortion portrayal as misleading and evasive. By their own accounts here the abortors are estranged, submissive and incoherent. They are estranged: detached from the rooted security of sure family bonds, unaccountable to persons trusted enough that their standards count, alienated individuals without a continuum of generations in which the hold an honored place.

They are submissive: ready to acquiesce in abuse and neglect by their men, inarticulate in the face of inquiry, unready to take care of themselves even after mistreatment. These women show noticeable hostility toward those who misuse them, but instead of coming forward more assertively they make impulsive gestures that do almost nothing to establish their own responsibility, almost nothing that would make them persons to reckon with. Instead of standing up to those who victimize them, by an almost pathetic misdirection they assert their dominance over a creature the lies at their disposal. Just as child battering misdirects parental hostility, away from those dominating persons who are its source and toward others who are helpless, so abortion appears to deflect much rage and frustration. So repeatedly there is an aggravated helplessness in relation to someone stronger. And so continually that unhappy situation is more reinforced than relieved by abortion, which is an exercise of *incoherent* self-assertion, yet self- injuring and so victimizing. Violence begets more violence. Humiliation stoops instead of stiffening.

CHAPTER SEVEN
DISLOCATION OF PURPOSE

A theme that runs like a leitmotiv [a dominant and reoccurring theme] through these tales is incoherence. It establishes itself from the outset in the inexplicable way so many of the women came to be pregnant. Virtually every woman and man interviewed is competent in contraceptive procedures and has access to them. Every birth-control clinic has its in-house stories about contraceptive ignorance, like the one told of the woman who came in, astonished and pregnant, even though her boyfriend had had a vasectomy. He had even shown her the scar. Where? She pointed right under the armpit (f: 39).

But the women in these books are not backward or naive about how to contracept. Why, then, do they do it so ineptly? They are so haphazard about it as to seem almost purposeful. In a very few cases conception does result from outright contraceptive failure, no matter what the method. But more typical is the fifteen-year-old, youngest of all the group: "I was going with this guy, you know. It wasn't meant to happen, you know. And I wasn't ready for it. I wasn't using any sort of birth control. I don't know why not. I just wasn't.

We were screwing all the time, but I guess I just didn't think about getting pregnant" (F: 198). This girl was just emerging from her second abortion in three months.

One young woman, when the interviewer noticed that she hadn't seemed worried about pregnancy, mused that she was, "well, kind of ambivalent. [Conflicting feelings]. I think in a way I wanted to get pregnant." Why? "Sort of as self-punishment. I was in a kind of 'down' time. And also great curiosity about it. I find it very reassuring to know that I'm fertile" (G: 52).

Sandy, who at twenty-one seems not very wise and has had a hysterectomy in the aftermath of her abortion, claims her priest told her it was doubly wrong to use protection when having sex with her boyfriend. So she wouldn't; "At least I hadn't prepared myself to go to bed with the guy that I was going to marry." When her mate told her to go on the pill, "I told him that I just could not force myself to do that, because I felt it was wrong to prepare myself for a sexual relationship" (G: 129, 130) (this was after five years of sex).

A married woman of thirty, mother of two, who aborted the third, tells that after five years on the pill she began to suspect that it had made her sterile. She wondered, "What have I done? What has happened to my body? And I realized now that this was part of my getting pregnant. It only happened after the abortion: that I could really see: that I could really see there had been something to being able to say "Well, I can get pregnant. I haven't done myself irrevocable harm." (G: 114).

Another woman reminiscing about three abortions during her twenties: "The reason, ultimately, was because I was very self- destructive. But the reason at that time seemed to me that if I used my diaphragm I would be *admitting* to a kind of 'lack of spontaneity." You know, that if I didn't use a diaphragm, it was his fault, 'he forced me.' You know, 'I didn't plan it ahead of time.' I didn't take responsibility for it, you see." (G: 74).

Robin Terhine, thirty, single, with two abortions behind her: "I was totally irresponsible about birth control. It was like I was just waiting to be punished. I set myself up for a real shitty thing. I didn't go out to do it, but I didn't do anything to not make it happen. I'm always dangling with fate. I was all hot to get pregnant. I don't know what it is" (F: 65).

Hans Lehfeldt, NYU professor of OB-Gyn, discounts contraceptive failure in what he describes as willful exposure to unwanted pregnancy. "These patients have such ambivalent [conflicting] feelings about pregnancy that neither contraception nor pregnancy offers a solution.

They want both, so they alternate between contraception and exposure" (F: 149,150).

No single explanation would seem able to account for the curious want of attention to contraception among these women and men who eventually came to the drastic judgment that they did not want a child born of their conceiving. But there is a repeated dislocation of purpose, an implausible hazard even on the part of some who from the beginning had wanted nothing to do with children. One is not quite sure how to understand what "unwanted pregnancies" and "unwanted children" would be, when the very mechanism of wanting, the compass of purpose, has become so demagnetized.

CHAPTER EIGHT
THE SUBORDINATE FEMALE

One thing any of us needs in order to pursue our purposes, to define and to know our wants, is a healthy ego. There seems to be some kind of ego deficiency sapping the pursuits of the women that Katrina and Linda asked to explain themselves.

Francke cautions that some of the pregnancies were not nearly as haphazard as one might first think, especially among the older teenagers. " In a 1974 study, "The Resolution of Teenage First Pregnancies, 'fully 72 percent of the white teenagers and 32 percent of the blacks aged fifteen to nineteen interviewed said that they become pregnant to force a marriage.

Other teenagers, especially those who were mistreated or came from foster homes, said they were looking for a source of love in a baby, whether they had any affection for the father of a child or not. Another reason was the desire to set up their own household, while others felt that becoming pregnant and carrying the pregnancy to term made them feel more adult and mature.

Loneliness was another factor in the pregnancy decision and among lower-income teenagers the economic carrot of welfare payments to dependent children. For the student whose grades were poor, pregnancy provided a feeling of creative accomplishment, while for teenagers who are not as attractive as the others, pregnancy was a proof fecundity and sexual desirability" (F: 183)

As at least some of these women later realized, a child conceived amid stability will tend to draw people even more tightly together, but in an unstable situation pregnancy is a poor remedy; it can alienate rather than rally those who should be together. The women Francke describes are not schemers, or women of purpose; they seem somehow to be ricocheting through life.

So in the interviews. One is struck, for instance, by the hapless way many of them cling to men you wouldn't need your best friend to tell you were schlemiels. [A habitual bungler] There are teenage memories of how girls thought they had to be ready to yield to sex indiscriminately to the boys on demand, or else suffer rejection.

There is a persuasive acquiescence in these women that does not, however, seem to pass away with adolescence. For example, one meets a professional woman, divorced, with a daughter, living with an eighteen year old boy (ten years her junior) who kept walking out on her, yet by who she had two aborted pregnancies. (:51, 53).

In the matter of contraception, the women note very frequently that the men insisted that it was their-the woman's-responsibility. Despite the fact that female contraceptives are either hazardous to health, or elaborately cumbersome, it is interesting how often, with the woman's acquiescence;

[agreement without protest] the men refuse to use condoms for no other reason than their own convenience.

As one woman, the mother of eight, explained, "I guess we were just careless. My husband didn't want me to take pills. My mother has cancer and no one can prove the pills didn't cause it. The IUD? I'm not sold on them. Anything like that can cause something. And the diaphragm. My second one is a diaphragm baby.

So I leave it up to my husband and we both watch the calendar. He hates the rubber. He says it is like taking a shower with his boots on" (f: 97).

A husband explains, "She felt that it was a one-sided deal, that it was the woman who had to use birth control. I refuse to wear rubbers. Rubbers are very insensitive and putting them on is the fastest two-handed game in town" (F: 128); cf. G: 330).

Another man, veteran of nine abortions, feels similarly: "I can't stand wearing rubbers. It's like washing your feet with your socks on" (: f: 143).

And the two books are full of "postponed" vasectomies, enough to keep a clinic going for a year. I was reminded of a psychiatry professor I had years ago, who often told stories of his earlier obstetrics practice. Frequently, he recalled, couples would come in to have the wife's tubes tied. He would explain that this was a fairly tricky surgical operation and would recommend instead a vasectomy, which involved no health risk and was simple enough to be performed during an office call. The husbands always said they would think it over, but no couple ever returned. The male seems to dominate whenever given leave to do so.

The female counteraction to this pattern of male self-concern seems to be covert and even self-destructive. One mother of two, age thirty, got pregnant after the family had moved to accommodate a career opportunity for her husband, at the cost of her teaching position. "I had passed my thirtieth birthday a year before and here I was faced with – What am I going to do with my life? That's a very real question to deal with when you've just given up a job that you really like. And I think all of those feelings were tied up with why I got pregnant. I don't know whether one wants to say it was a kind of – almost hostility toward my husband, almost a subconscious anger that we had left where we were living. Although, in reality, we had discussed all of that" (G: 115).

Another woman, thirty two, mother of five, who had conceived during an unaffectionate episode, reflected: "maybe I was saying, 'All right, you bastard, I'll get pregnant and you'll have to pay for it.' " (F: 105).

CHAPTER NINE
ACQUIESCENT YET ANGRY

The decision to abort is frequently tinctured by a strange acquiescence- [agreement without protest]-cum-anger. One youngster, married a year and now pregnant at eighteen, was faced by her hostile in-laws, who had opposed the marriage and, believing that a baby would preserve it, told the young couple to move out in two weeks if they hadn't had an abortion. "I love the baby. I love my husband. I just think it would be better for him if I have the abortion. I'll get over it. I'm sure there'll be a lot of times when I'll have to think about it, but we got so many problems now. So many. I know I can have another baby someday. But it's this one I love now. I just love her so much.... But my mother-in-law says we got to be off the farm in two weeks—if I keep on having my baby" (F: 95).

Another, about to undergo for a second time a second-trimester abortion, says, "My boyfriend and I decided on an abortion because Andy is going through a divorce and it would have put another trauma on him. This is harder for him than me. He just didn't want a baby. I really did want it, because I don't think I could mentally handle the abortion, but he talked me into going to Planned Parenthood" (F: 85).

One girl (one of only two interviewees not to choose abortion) lived years in a fantasy romance with her high school hero-sweetheart who went off to college leaving her pregnant and who, the very night she eventually gave birth to their daughter, was off in Canada in bed with another girl because he "needed somebody" (G:413). She describes her relationship with him: "I wasn't too upset about people finding out. In a way I was kind of proud of it. Because I was having David's baby.... It was also kind of an ego thing for me, because David was very popular in high school. Everybody knew David and liked David. And so people used to look up to me, you know, because David cared about me. And the fact that I would be having his baby was kind of impressive, I thought." (G:389)   She also describes her father and mother: Through this whole thing, anything my father said, she went along. She is completely submissive. That's a whole big thing that has to do with my relationship with my mother, too. Anything my father says is right. And so she went along with him" (G: 389)

It is there in so many of the women: an absence of personal strength, which Judith bardwick and others have commented on. "I flew home and thought maybe I'd get married instead, but both of the guys I had been sleeping with said they didn't feel like it and didn't want the responsibility. They both convinced me I should have the abortion. I wasn't very assertive then" (F: 89).

"My husband, I don't think was as much concerned, perhaps as I was. Maybe I-(laughs) you know, maybe I'm a little insecure" (G: 334).

And a sixteen year old: "I get scared real easy, you know. Like I was scared to call that counseling number. You know? It just scared me. Over nothing! Just calling a telephone number! I-I was afraid to do it. And-I don't know, he didn't decide- I didn't even know he was gonna to go with me 'til we were talking to the Reverend and he was saying, 'Fly to New York' and 'You get this and that.' Stig says, you know, 'Yeah, I'm gonna go with her.' And I think, "Whoa! Far out!' You know. But I didn't say, 'Oh *before* you weren't gonna go with me.' You know, 'cause he would have been pretty embarrassed" (G: 219). The women repeatedly display an unreadiness to assert themselves, to claim fair and fond consideration from their men. Instead, they are uncannily submissive.

CHAPTER TEN
THE VANISHING MALE

As things developed, many women learned that when they became pregnant they found themselves alone. Sometimes the boyfriend would simply hang up the phone. Or he would find some other way to back away. "My boyfriend is twenty-one. I called him this morning, but no one answered. He said he didn't know if he had the time to come with me for the abortion. If he won't be at the house tomorrow before nine I'm going to leave him a note saying don't bother to see me again. I'm going to be bold" (F: 185, 86).

One young man whose girlfriend, after eight years on-again-off again and two abortions, won't speak to him, remembers: "When she went for the abortion, I wasn't around. It was frightening to me. I made excuses that I had to be at football practice or something, but in reality it was fear that kept me away. I felt guilty for a long time" (F: 146).

And a woman who had had an earlier abortion experience with her husband before their marriage recollects how terrible the isolation was. "I can remember just sitting in my apartment on my sofa bed and just not wanting to move.

I was aware that some terrible wave of malfunctioning thing was coming over me that I needed help....The abortion really was a catalyst that made me start dealing with a lot of shit. I was angry at Billy, I had deep-rooted anger at my sister for always bossing me around and this time being wrong and there were financial problems. My sister had borrowed money for the abortion and Billy wasn't paying her back, but was going out and buying furniture for his apartment" (F: 174).

The resentment of the men is there, but it is so muted. Said one woman: "I think it's going to change our relationship a little. Like he was telling me, it's your fault you're pregnant. You should have done something about it. It's not all my fault. He could have done something about it too. He just says it's up to the girl and I don't like that at all -- -- -- he knows that I feel hostile to him right now. He tries to do nice things and I ignore them. I couldn't be nice back. He told me to call him at home after this thing tonight. I don't even know if I want to talk to him"F: 188).

Rarer is the woman who, at forty-one, was looking back across two decades at her abortion and what she considered a very destructive experience: "That was the end of my trust in people. Really, to a great extent. When I saw that both my husband and my father came through at the last minute, when it was safest is to do it – that was it. I have never really trusted anyone since" (G: 264).

One has the impression that the pregnancy crisis and abortion disclosed rather than caused the falling away of friends and mates. In case after case there seem to have been no previous bonds generous and giving enough –despite the frequency with which they were anointed as "caring" and "loving" – to sustain much claim on either good sense or energetic support. In so many instances the woman simply woke up to find that they had been on their own all along, despite all the couplings. When the emergency erupts, bonds that have been long frayed and rotted simply snap.

CHAPTER ELEVEN
ALIENATION FROM PARENTS

One of the very typical responses to this isolation is a repeated unwillingness to confront those who oppose. Parents appear most often in this opponent' role, but the trait is not limited to dealing with them. With a rythmetic frequency, almost that of a refrain, these women describe how unbearable it would have been to suffer parental disapproval or disagreement. "If my parents were dead, then I'd have that baby. But they're here to remind me of guilt and lay on their disapproval. They're lovely people really, and practice what they preach" (F: 61).

One boyfriend senses it: "She feels if she does go ahead and have the baby, she's going to miss out on a lot. She wants to go to college and she can't face telling her mom and dad. That's the worst thing" (F: 117).

Mothers in particular loom large. "There's no reason to tell my mother about it. She'd have a fit. She'll never know" (F: 201).

"My mother doesn't know I'm here. She's sick and she's been sick for a long time. She didn't know about the first abortion either. I can't tell her because I wouldn't want to upset her. She'd have a fit. I don't think she'd allow me to have an abortion anyway. She's make me have the baby and then give it up for adoption. If I went through the nine months I wouldn't want to give it up. That's how she had me (F: 190, 91).

I tried to talk to her when I was thinking of having an abortion, but she don't agree with it and she got kind of mad when I was trying to tell her, so I'm going to have to think about what I'm going to tell her after I've had the abortion" (F:57).

"I also have a very strict mother who once told me, in high school, that should I ever get in trouble, just keep going, because she never wanted to see me again" (G:128).

And another girl remembered, "I finally broke down and told her....She called me every name she could think of—bitch, whore, slut—which made me feel really terrific" (F:84).

Fathers too are difficult to face in this situation. Several of the mothers concealed their daughter's pregnancy from them. "My father would be shocked if he knew I had slept with anybody. My older sister ran away from home at eighteen. He doesn't speak about her at all. He's very bitter. I was scared' (F: 199).

For some women, to open this antagonized subject up with their parents would jeopardize the independence they had striven for. "I had made a huge point of not taking any financial assistance from my father after I graduated from college and I was not about to admit to him that I had made any mistake about anything. It would have been awful to have that child" (F: 230).

Oddly, this same woman later remarks, "I didn't resent our families for causing us to have the abortion, but then I've always been low on resentment" (F: 232).

Another gives her predicament: "It would have meant going home to my parents who would-would help me but-it would crush my grandparents. And definitely everyone in the town would talk. This sort of thing. I don't know how I would be supporting myself; probably to this day I would be depending on my parents for help. It would have meant not being able to finish college. It would have meant a lot of things. I don't know whether-they probably would have encouraged me to give the child up. Although I think they would have supported me in whatever I, you know, finally decided to do" (G: 53, 54).

As might be anticipated the parents here described reacted in a variety of ways. Some hastened their daughters off to abortion clinics before the daughters had given that idea much thought. Others seemed more concerned for themselves, or were preoccupied with how they must have raised their child badly. Still others had little council to give and simply agreed to whatever their daughter intended to do; in some of the stories one senses more ennui [boredom] than real support. Some shouted and cursed. But many – very many – simply were never approached. Whatever the outcome, there appears to be a high degree of the alienation between these women and their parents, such that they were not often willing to ask their parents in on the crisis. As Francke puts it:

"Among the black women I interviewed, some had abortions in spite of their mothers' willingness to take the child.

Others had abortions because their mothers wouldn't agree to raise the baby.

Among the white women, the role of the parent was more abstract. Over and over again the single women of all ages would admit that they didn't want their parents even to know about their abortion for fear it would hurt them. Although they agreed that the alternative, having the child, would hurt them more. These women didn't give their parents the option to support or reject them. Isolating themselves, the white middle-class single women made their decision alone. "They wouldn't understand" was a recurring phrase. 'They don't ever need to know' was another" (F: 47).

It is as she says. The interviews reveal very few women whose maturity stood them well enough to allow a confrontation with parents over this most heartfelt of family dilemmas, with any hope of an agreeable finale.

CHAPTER TWELVE
RESENTMENT OF THOSE CLOSEST

Francke does interview a number of parents of abortees. There are some interesting points to be seen in these conversations. Most of the parents are very solicitous for their children. This arises partly from her sample, which is composed almost exclusively of parents who were accompanying their children through the abortion procedure and so would not represent the more antagonized. One suspects that the young women may, because of their lack of forthrightness, be painting a prejudiced picture of their parents and may be reporting their reactions as somewhat more irrational then they really were. There is reason to question the fairness and candor of the abortion seekers in their accounts of persons who do not offer them unqualified support.

In fact, there is a pattern of need for this support. The women find themselves facing a disaster which, if not uncourted, is at least now unwelcome. They sense inadequate resources of their own to see it through and look frantically to find who is standing by them. Often there is no one, at least no one of close kinship or friendship. It is a telltale time and their demand for support is peremptory and urgent.

But many of these women were stung when they encounter rebuffs. One mother of two went to her own obstetrician to ask for an abortion, but was told that in Massachusetts he could not legally perform one at the time. He referred her to Planned Parenthood, who sent her to Pregnancy Counseling Service, who put her in touch with an abortionist in New York, who put her in bed for weeks with a perforated uterus and intestine. "What made me angry was that my own doctor, who's very competent – he's the head of obstetricians at the hospital – that he couldn't help me out. Morally he would have, but legally he couldn't. And I know this wouldn't have happened if he had done the abortion. And that's what made me angry. That I had to go and be in someone else's hands, that I knew nothing about, just because I – well – made a mistake and was pregnant" (G:102). One doctor, called on to repair the wreckage of another's botched abortion, said to the woman: "'I guess you know it's all over,' and all I could think of was don't be like that. Be nicer to me. Help me. I felt really bad I couldn't stop crying" (F: 80).

One woman in her early twenties encountered a put down from a priest. "After the whole thing was over, I felt very repentant and I wanted to cleanse myself of my sins. And, you know, 'God has punished me for this horrible sin. I went to a priest and he said, "well, my dear, but you're excommunicated"! You have committed one of the unforgivable sins of the church and you have to go through the Bishop or the Pope,' or something like that. I just said, to hell with it! That's it and that was the end of my contact, really, with the church. I mean, that they could say that to me... in fact, the very fact that they reject me, on the point of this abortion, seems ludicrous to me" (G:149 ,50).

Was the priest insensitive and abusive, or was he telling her this was no petty item she claimed to be confessing? One has no access to his recollection of the encounter. In a sense, though, many of these women feel excommunicated on all sides, at the very time they most crave communion.

If one of the male partners gives a clue that some of this experience may have been provoked by the women themselves. He had been opposed to the abortion, but did not discuss his feelings "because it might upset her." He has tried to keep from her how strongly he had been against it. "I was against her for a while, two. Sally is basically a very, very sweet person. She does the things you like to do, because she wants to make you happy. But during the period that she found out she was pregnant, and then she had the abortion, and then for three or four weeks afterwards, she was an entirely different person. She was hard to get along with; she never wanted to do anything. She didn't want to talk about anything and she acted as if she didn't want me to be around -- -- -- -- there wasn't any physical hostility, but the mental hostility was there. It was as if we both hated each other, because when she found out she was pregnant, you would gather that I had done something wrong to her " (F: 163).

One woman herself tells how it was: "when I got pregnant, suddenly my husband and I weren't getting along so well. I was real touchy and oversensitive and I didn't feel so good either. My husband wasn't giving me anything I needed, so we decided to get divorced" (F: 110).

Another woman, supported by a man other than the one who had impregnated her, recalls: "he was hurt by the way I behaved, he said, because I didn't sort of really take him into it and I didn't feel that he was -- -- -- -- I mean, to say that he wasn't supportive is not true because he was, terribly. But my feeling, I think, stemmed mostly from resentment. You know, that he wasn't the person who conceived the child, he wasn't the person who had to have the abortion and as such could not possibly understand what I was going through. So, the closer it came, the nastier I got" (D: 42).

CHAPTER THIRTEEN
WOMEN AND MEN SET AT ODDS

Other women recollected that their resentment festered over their mates' decision not to oppose them. "I was hurt even though the abortion was my idea and it was the only thing to do. I guess I wanted him to talk me out of it, to reassure me we could make it. Instead he was cold. I wish he could have been more feeling" (F: 96).

And another: "sometimes I blame him for having let me go through with it. I think he should have said we could have made it with another baby. We made a selfish decision" (F: 100).

And another: "the night after my pregnancy was confirmed, my husband and I went out to dinner and my only emotion was anger. I was angry that I was going to have an abortion. He could have persuaded me not to have it, but he didn't. So I wanted him to talk me out of it, I also didn't want him to. But in the back of my mind I wanted to be able to escape from him, to get divorced, to leave him, just to go home alone. I did not want to feel trapped" (F: 107).

And in their own confused state of attention and expectation a good number of the women seem to have misconstrued the concern and puzzlement and that there men did have towards them. As one of them told it, "the guy harbored deep resentment about it. There was this funny little edge in everything he did and I thought he'd thought that the sooner I had the abortion the better. We never really disgust it. It was just understood that I'd have an abortion. He was just kind of a little cruel to me. I've never consider myself an emotionally mature person and to me it was a rejection thing. It never occurred to me that he was upset that I was having this abortion. It never, never occurred to me. I didn't find out until a year and a half later that he had been very, very upset. He felt rejected and felt that I would never, never have a child of his, that I did not consider him suitable for me and that it was pointless to love me")F: 53).

The story conventionally told by women is that their men were of less help than they had hoped: they faltered, they drew apart, they were unthoughtful, they left the women on their own. From the men another story emerges: that the men were highly concerned, who were finding it difficult to read what the women were feeling and stifle their own preferences precisely in order to provide the woman with the autonomy they seemed to want. One father's is typical: "I would rather it not happen, but I don't want to run in and stop it, because it's her body and it's her free will -- -- -- -- so I just gotta accept what's happening. If she decided at the last moment not to do it, I would be feeling fantastic" (F: 120).

Another man, one of the most deeply moved among all interviewed, later grieved over the abortion and his assent to it.

She said, "Shall I have an abortion?" and I said, "I guess so," she made all the arrangements for a week later. The whole week I was extremely jumpy and preoccupied. People at work kept asking me why I was so preoccupied. I kept twirling the decision over and over in my head. A lot had to do with the women's movement, which my wife was a part and which presumed a woman's ability to go out and make a good living without being trapped down by the familial obligations. I felt this child would hurt that. She was just beginning to ascend in a good and important job. Pregnancy and all the things that go with it would have knocked the shit out of her career, it just having taken off after the birth of our second child. (After the abortion) I tried to tend to her. I didn't need tending to. I hadn't had an abortion. She didn't need me at that point doing a boo-hoo act. She needed help for herself. In retrospect I think a lot of damage was done to our marriage. My fault was in not articulating sooner than it was a child of mine I wanted born. Mostly I was responsive to her life -- -- -- --in a sense I blame her for the abortion. Without her requirements for a career, the pregnancy would never have been an issue. I would have said, "F---k it." I love kids. But there was an intensity about the moment regarding women and careers. I paid too much attention to that and not to what I wanted. I don't know how she would have reacted if I'd said this was a child of mine and I wanted it. Instead, I lost control of my own will and didn't see how much it would affect me. (F: 130–32)

His statement seems worthy of long quotation because it presents such an ironic inversion of the inequities and silent frustrations that give birth to the women's movement. And it recurs in these books. The male senses he is left out; the female, that she is not being supported. She says he wouldn't come with her; he, that she went off without him.

Linda Bird Francke acknowledges: "The right to abdicate future motherhood is guaranteed. The right to insist on future fatherhood is not. And to some men, that is very disturbing and unfair" (F: 114).

It also raises questions about a program developed in an Oakland counseling center for males involved in their partners abortions and the men were advised to be unquestioningly supportive during the near aftermath of abortion and only afterwards to encourage their women to talk about it. They were told to expect and to absorb hostility for some time and then to take the initiative in adopting contraception when their sex life resumed, as a way of assuring the woman that they, the men, didn't want the women have to go through another abortion)F: 115).

This kind of counseling urges the male to be tenderly supportive of what must be an essentially female decision and experience. It may however, keep him at a stranger's distance. Even more, like many counseling programs it may be more intended to alleviate symptoms of distress than to discern what is wrong underneath: coping, not curing.

There seems no reason to believe that the testimony of the male partners in Francke book (Maxtone–Graham interviews only women) is any less representative than that of the many women whose stories appear. Yet these men seem solicitous, sympathetic, accommodating and, at the same time, puzzled by the degage [disengaged] hostility of the women. They are stymied by it to the point where their own interests are muted -- -- only to emerge later, suffused with anger. These accounts, ironically at variance with the impressions of the women, need not cause any reader to disbelieve what the women narrate, but ought to temper the way they are to be understood.

There seems to be some sort of hostility at work which alienates women choosing abortion from even the helpful enjoyment of whatever intimate trust they had previously (and possibly unrealistically) thought they shared with their kinfolk and mates.

A decision is produced -- apparently the result of freshly independent and straightforward the deliberation -- yet shadowed by much unspoken and undigested thought. Then it is rushed to completion without the sharing of minds and hearts one would hope for even in matters of far less importance.

CHAPTER FOURTEEN
A CHOICE OF MUDDLED CHOOSING

Free and autonomous choice is so valued a feature of the abortion experience that it deserves to be inquired after as purposefully as these stories will allow. One thing quickly noticed is the pattern way which some of the women tended to assigned to others the blame for their unhappy predicament. It is a trait one would more readily expect to find in very young women and Francke does cite findings to this effect: "Upon learning that she is pregnant, such a teenager is apt to express extensive denial, including disclaiming any responsibility on her part for her pregnancy. She cannot see herself as a mother nor can she see the fetus as a baby. As for the abortion, she accepts it for herself, but does not condone it for others" (F: 180). That incoherence again.

But incoherent seems not to be a monopoly of teenagers. The woman mentioned earlier, who decided upon abortion because she had been independent since college days ("and I was not about to admit to him that I had made any mistake about anything") and later observed that she "didn't resent our families for causing us to have this abortion" (F: 230, 232), was 62 years old when interviewed, looking back over

40 years at her abortion. She makes the families "responsible" for what she was unwilling to tell them. Martha Mueller, a Brooklyn Planned Parenthood counselor, sees this as a repeating pattern.

Francke summarizes her thoughts:

Some think that the legalization of abortion has opened a Pandora's Box of faulty decision-making. When abortion was illegal there was a common enemy in the form of the law. Now that abortion is primarily a matter of choice, the decision rests squarely on the shoulders of the woman, a decision many would rather not take the responsibility for. Some blame their husbands or boyfriends for "forcing" them to have the abortion. Others point the finger at their parents, who have insisted on the abortion or who, the patients maintain, would be furious if they found out their daughter was pregnant. Often it's the doctor who takes the "blame" for the abortion. "He did it to me" is a phrase heard often in clinical hospital corridors when the doctor walks by. "That's just moving the responsibility," says Mueller. "Women are very good at that.")F: 32)

The stories lend substance to her observation. One woman, married with two teenage children, is a medical student now and at age thirty-four has gone in for her second abortion. "I was angry. God had to do this again? -- - - I was furious, furious, furious. He (her husband) likes to call all the shots, but never to carry them out. I was absolutely furious at him and made him do all the dirty work. I disclaimed any responsibility for the pregnancy. I felt I was absolved of all this. He should have had that vasectomy. I was totally irrational." And then she muses, "The resentment didn't go away. I kept thinking that this was something not everyone has to go through, so why should I. My husband should have said, "I'm definitely going to have a vasectomy."

In the same way I should have said, "I'm going to have my tubes tied." But I haven't. And he hasn't. We all play such destructive games" (F: 107,108).

Another woman, thirty, whose teenage abortion had been followed by a miscarriage and then years of infertility, grieved: "I blamed my husband for making me have the abortion. How could he have done this to me? Our marriage began to fall apart." But earlier she had described how the decision was made: "my sister and Randy and I sat down to talk about it. One of them, I can't remember which, said I should have an abortion. I have a background of not making decisions for myself, but I still said I didn't want to have an abortion. Randy said he wanted to marry me, but he just wasn't ready for children at that time. He just couldn't take on that responsibility. I kind of went along and agreed" (F: 78, 81). The young man's reason for urging the abortion is not very impressive, but it is not that different from what motivates most of the abortions in these stories. And characteristically, after a process of muddled collaboration, he is assigned responsibility for the decision.

It is not always the "Randy" who is blamed. Like God, society sometimes serves as an indistinct bogeyman. After two abortions, a marriage and divorce, VD, and then a third abortion after a one night stand, one woman complained of "great resentment that society was pushing me into feeling that I had to get rid of the child because I was not married -- feeling that I was being pushed by society's values around me, by the social stigma, not to have a child because I was not married" (G. 68).

One highly confused woman in her middle twenties tells of her abortion at age nineteen. She first describes how it was that she conceived. "I don't like to use birth control. I feel like it sort of destroys the power of my fertility. I don't know how to explain that. But at one time I tried the pill and it made me real sick and I didn't want to have an IUD 'cause I think they're very dangerous. So I was using a diaphragm, but I wasn't really using it. A diaphragm makes me feel like I have to keep my cervix or my reproductive organs away from everything" (F: 86).

She then had a saline abortion, with no account of any particular ill treatment and looked back:

Mostly I felt real brutalized, like I'd been treated like a piece of shit by the nurses and by the hospital and by the doctors. Now I want to have a baby. First of all, I'm more stable than I used to be. I have more of an understanding. The reason I had my abortion was because I was a poor working class woman who was trying to go to school. There's just no way I could have that child. It was society. We live in an anti poverty society where my having a child would have totally ruined whatever aspirations I had. I had no choice. A lot of times we talk about a woman's rights and I do think we have a right to choose whether or not to have children. But for many of us our class and our economic background pretty much makes the choice for us. We really don't have the free choice to have children when we want them. But right now I would really like to have a child in spite of it. I feel like caring for another human being and seeing this little human being born and raising it and fighting for this person to survive. It also makes you a stronger person. (F: 88).

Among the approximately 100 abortions accounted for in these books, there are very, very few that appear to have been imposed upon the women. Yet there is widespread feeling of having been victimized. The phrase "had to have" is a repeating prefix to abortion in the vocabulary.

Abortion arrives somehow as an imperative associated with outside forces. It may be that even in cases where a woman is in sole and apparently sovereign control of the decision, there is some dislocation, some short-circuit in that decision experience that leaves her without a full sense of having done a free thing, of having taken her life in her own hands. It is also possible that there is something so denying, so negative -- even destructive – in abortion that it is a wrench to have to realize that one has chosen it. Abortion is said to be a symbolically prime choice for a women in our time, yet these stories suggest that it is backed into or backed away from, rather than decisively chosen and later ratified.

CHAPTER FIFTEEN
HOSTILITY TO FATHER, HOSTILITY TO CHILD

These interviews make it difficult to figure out how the male partner participates with (or against) the woman who is struggling with an abortion decision. Much less muddled is the way in which the man enters that decision, not as a codeliberant, but as the one whose relationship with her begets her relationship to the child she is carrying. Francke correctly states "The most critical factor in the decision to abort -- is the relationship with the male partner" (F: 47).

In some cases a baby is unwanted, not because its father is unwanted, but simply because the man – woman bond is not felt to be strong enough to become a father – mother one. "We're still too early in our relationship to be tied together" (F: 157).

"My husband and I were fighting about everything and I didn't want to have this baby and bring it up alone. I also thought I might resent the baby because I resented its father so much. I felt bad because all my life I'd wanted to have a baby and suddenly I couldn't have this one. I hated him" (F: 110).

More often, though, the child of a man disliked or distrusted falls under the same judgment. By what the psychologist call a displacement of affect the women fail to develop an independent bond with the child carried and instead intrude upon the child the hostility they feel towards the begetting male. "God, you have no idea how much I hated him. And I sure in hell was not going to have that child. I had the abortion to hurt him primarily" (F: 241). "I remember thinking it was impossible to have another child especially one of George's -- don't even remember discussing the pregnancy with George -- it was part of my shtick not to need him then" (F: 105)

A young woman whose surfer-type boyfriend grouched at her one night went off the next night and slept with another man, then returned. She was interviewed at the abortion clinic, trying to determine the age of the fetus, to determine which of the men was the father. Said the surfer, "we don't believe in abortion, really, but she didn't want to have the baby of someone she didn't love and was only with for a night" (F: 118).She found it was the boyfriends baby but went ahead with the abortion anyway.

One teenager doesn't regret her abortion: "I don't know we really weren't getting along that good because being pregnant's a hassle. I was sick to my stomach that I was really bitchy" (G: 203).

Another woman, mother of two, had lost her job when the family moved to help her husband's career: "what also came out was how I did not want this pregnancy. I got into this situation and the reasons we're beginning to appear. I mean,

I wouldn't have been able to guess that my hostile feelings toward my husband for having moved here-- were at work" (G: 118).

A woman in her twenties, who now has decided never to bear children, looks back "I never thought about the fetus -- it was something that belongs there and had no place in my life at that time. I'd hated it before the abortion, but mostly I hated the man" (F: 50).

One who underwent two abortions says of the second, "because I was more ambivalent about this baby, being fonder of the father, I waited till I was over two months pregnant -- I was more upset about losing that baby than the one before. I thought both before and after the abortion that maybe I should have married the father" (G: 233 – 34).

It is a thing sensed by the men too. One of them put it clearly: "the only man that can totally agree to an abortion is a guy who's just dating a girl he doesn't feel anything about. If he has any feeling at all about her, I would hope that he wouldn't agree to it. If a man loves a woman, I don't think he would agree to it under any circumstances" (F: 164).

The stories do not quite bare him out, since there does seem to be decisions to abort when mother and father are ostensibly at one. But under more positive circumstances the offspring seems to have a better chance of surviving. One woman who bore her child explained, "I was proud I was having David's baby" (G: 389).

Occasionally the alienation helps rather than blocks the mother-sense. A black woman whose husband had walked out on her when she was carrying their first child and then did it again during her next pregnancy admitted: "I was considering having an abortion then, but I couldn't. I kind of fell in love with the baby. His walking out made me closer to my two year old and the unborn child" (F: 67).

For some women there seems to be almost a disability to establish any bond with the unborn except by borrowing, so to speak, from their relationship of the father. Allison, looking back at three abortions when she was in her twenties, says of the first: "this was a man who, besides everything else, was physically repulsive to me. It was a very sick relationship and I was a very unhappy person. And at the time that I got pregnant my immediate response was one of utter disgust-- I had no sense, really, of the fact that I was pregnant with a child. It was much more as if I had a growth, or a tumor that I just wanted to get rid of and I didn't want anybody to know about it because it was so "disgusting"." Now that she is thirty two and living with another man, she admits, "I'm not particularly into marrying him, or getting married right now, either. But if I were to become pregnant by him, I think that I'd be very happy and thrilled at the idea of having a child, because he's a beautiful person. And he's exactly kind of man whose child I would like to have." In retrospect, viewing her three abortions, she explains: "it was very real to want to have a child them. But not those children. And those children were defined by my emotional state and by the man I was involved with and everything else. I mean it wasn't like I was saying, "I don't ever want to have a child," it was, "I don't want to have *this* child." For whatever reasons" (G: 70, 82, and 87).

CHAPTER SIXTEEN
WOMEN DISENGAGED

The readiness to disengage from one's offspring at unpleasant moments is not limited to pregnant women, as any parent knows who has been told by his or her spouse, "your son wrecked the car last night," or, "your daughter tells me she just flunked out of school." But what functions in these abortion situations seems to be more serious and more ambivalent, to use a Francke title term. One senses a persistently weak ability both to differentiate and to ally. For example, many of the women testify that it was in the critical emergency of undesired pregnancy that they came to a more conscious awareness of their own autonomy. The decision to abort is seen by them as an assertion of rights that had been previously gone unrespected and ignored – by themselves and by others. On other hand, very few of the women seem interested in pursuing the issue of rights.

There is meager talk of the rights of grandparents, husbands, or sexual partners and virtually none of the possibly countervailing rights of the unborn. Girls who are angry at their parents and struggling to disassociate their own welfare from their parental authority seemed particularly unable to view their own offspring as having any identity with which they themselves should have to come to terms. Women who exert themselves to claim respect for their careers, their health, or their persons from mates who had taken them for granted appear to be unconscious of any correlative claims on them by their own young

The women speaking here are wary. They have been disappointed in their closest relationships, those of affection and kinship and commitment, which create for people the security of home. Somehow these women have not found – or forged – bonds that are firm attachments yet allow a desirable elasticity of freedom. Most of us find satisfaction when we can count on these closest loyalties as unquestionably secure. It is this commitment to honor claims, to be prepared to sacrifice, to expect to forfeit preference in many ways that must be balanced with the freedom to extend one's reach to the fullest length of personal maturity and fulfillment. The women in these two books seem not to enjoy such a balance.

Lacking the guarantees of their own individuality, they are weak to acknowledge it in others. Deprived of secure attachment, they seem somehow handicapped in offering it. The unborn, at cost of his or her life, seems to suffer from a failure of personal bonding that the mother also experiences with her parents and with her mate(s), and perhaps with her other children as well. As one woman, describing her own abortion decision two years into her marriage put it: "that child would have been so f----d up because I was f----d up. Billy was so f----d up, our financial scene was so bad. Everything about our lives was so crazy and so unsettled and so unresolved that a child probably would have been so resented and so not treated well that he would've gotten the shit end of the stick" (F: 175).

CHAPTER SEVENTEEN
REASONS FOR NOT WANTING A CHILD

Obviously, hostility towards a child's father, though salient, is not the only motive or reason which drew these women to wish not to give birth. What are the other reasons? Some, of course, are frivolous. Francke tells of one very young girl who "decided on an abortion because it was football season and a pregnancy would interfere with her baton twirling" (F: 180).

Some are openly and simply selfish. "There was no question about this pregnancy. I really don't want the hassle. I don't want to be bothered with a baby and that's the cold, hard truth. I'm simply not interested in bringing one up. Four years ago, yes but not now. I don't even like babies. Keep them away from me. They are a drag" (F: 169).

One man interviewed was an abortion veteran: three apiece by his two wives and three by others. Says he, "I wanted to create a home life, but that didn't include children. I wanted to be the center of attention -- what terrified me about having children was that it entailed for me a commitment not to reject them. And I still craved attention for myself" (F: 143, 145). His second wife had her own reasons for not wanting to have children by him: "She already had two children by her first marriage and was determined not to have any by me so that I'd be a better father to her children" (F: 144). A good number of the married couples explain that before they married they had agreed they did not want any children. One wife says that whenever she had a pregnancy scare, "I went through a lot of hell considering it. I wasn't too sure exactly why. But the idea was that I would be absolutely trapped, that my life would end. I never knew any little kids. I never knew any babies, or children. So it was completely foreign to me. And – it scared me. And there would be days, I do recall, when I thought, "my God, if I get pregnant, I swear I'll take my bare hands and – claw it out." I really felt that way. Just (make scraping noise) dig it out" (G: 156).

Some of the explanations are difficult to follow and reflect an inner confusion. One woman explains: "with the pressure of the population explosion and feeling very sensitive to the social situation – that is, of bringing another child into the world – there were a lot of questions to weigh" (G: 114). She also mentions hostility against her husband because the family had recently moved to further his career. Now that her children are of school age there is a question of her own interests to resolve. When she comes to describe the actual decision to abort, however, she is somewhat incoherent. "Our decision was really made on our strengths. For me, it was a matter of having enough confidence in myself as a human being to be able to say: I know that I'll have feelings afterward. How can anybody not? Feeling empty, feeling – but I will cope with these feelings. I don't need to hide from them. I'm pregnant now, but, my God, will bring a child into the world simply because I am too afraid of having to face my feelings? No, we're too strong -- - what happened was an error and I'm going to undo it. And undo it out of my feeling of strength" (G: 120 – 21).

Then, too, there is the Budapest woman (F: 227) who, with two daughters already, had an illegal abortion during the Russian occupation of Hungary because the family was having such a desperate time trying to survive financially. The most peculiar feature of her story is that they were able to pay $10,000 in gold to have the abortion performed.

Some married couples give no reason for their decision other than "a baby just didn't fit in" (F: 151), or, "it's the wrong time for us to have a child. We've talked a lot about having a family and it will be another year or so -- it's not financial, it's just the desire. There would be great interference at this point in our lives. We're both in training positions. I'm a nurse and John is a psychologist. We are in a very highly pressured environment in our work situations right now and we feel even though we would like to have a child at some point, we would like to be ready to devote the time to it" (F: 152).

As one would anticipate, career requirements, especially for the woman, are often mentioned as a rationale for the decision to abort." she didn't want to have a baby because of her career as a model. She's doing commercials and she wants to make a lot of money and if she had a baby it would sort of put a stop to those plans" for (F: 119). "She wanted to go to school and she's working too and having the baby would mess the whole plan up. "'cause she'd have to come out of school and since she's so far in it, it wouldn't make no sense in her coming out, for in a year or so she'd be out of school, she'd have a steady job, we'd have our finances together. Get us a good budget and we'll see about having a baby them" (F: 124).

Sometimes it is the husband's career as much as the wife's which is the key factor. This was the case with a couple living in England where he was in medical school and she in graduate studies. "Then suddenly he was accepted at medical school (in Connecticut). And she decided to stay in England to finish up her masters before joining him. Rather than face the complicated mess, they decided it was not the time to have a child. And she had an abortion" (F: 219).

In other instances a child is unwelcome because of the financial implications, "our whole life-style would've been changed. I mean, you buy new furniture – and this all sounds very materialistic but that's not just it. It's your whole way of life. You know, you get involved in things. I was taking violin lessons and I was taking courses and I finally – you know – was out of the mess. I'm not a very good housekeeper; I was brought up in Europe with a lot of servants and I - it just – it would just have changed my life completely; and that's not the way I wanted it)" (G: 7).

As another explained it, "I was going to school at night and I have a garden, and I keep busy, and I just didn't want any more children-- -- we like to do outdoor things and this is impossible with a baby, canoeing and camping and things like that. So I just feel that it's better for me and it's better for the children and better for my husband" (G.: 94, 104).

Francke quotes a Planned Parenthood staffer who observes, "The older you are, especially for women who already have children and aren't desperately strapped for money, the heart of the decision is. For women have completed their ideal family size, the decision to abort can be excruciating. It's a life–style choice and we're not taught to think in such a self centered way" (F: 92 – 93).

Increasingly shared, evidently, is an understanding of what an "ideal family size" would be. "The population people have really gotten to me. And I feel very strongly about population control. I just can't see people having more than two children. Also, I know personally, for myself, that emotionally and psychologically it's better for me not to have more than two children. I – I can give just so much. I feel I've reached my limit" (G: 281).

Another mother of two emphasizes, "I couldn't deal with another one. I had too many oranges in the air. I care so much about children that they are an enormous burden. I just couldn't go through another one and do graduate school besides" (F: 105).

Those two women were, at the time of their abortions, twenty five and thirty two years old respectively. Another, the mother of three says I was thirty nine which is not, I feel, time to bear more children. My husband was forty two so this has something to do with our feeling about "our families complete and we'd don't want to start raising new babies" (G: 230).

For some women, their physical condition has sapped their ability to cope. "At first my husband wanted to keep it, but as the weeks went by and the morning sickness got so bad I couldn't take care of our little girl, he changed his mind. She is just beginning to crawl" (F: 99).

Another mother had a much longer history of misfortune: "I've been pregnant seven times in my life and only have one living child. My daughter Jennifer died five years ago and I had three miscarriages before that and two since. I swore with the last one I would never put my feelings on the line again. We had moved to Lexington from Chicago had rented a house with an extra bedroom so we could try again. But I miscarried again. I can remember lying in the hospital listening as nurses brought all the babies out to their mothers and I made the decision if I ever got pregnant again I would have an abortion" (F: 109).

One of the most poignant cases is that of a poor woman (not the only one we encounter) who remembered having abused her own child. "I put my hands around her throat like that. And I was just within an ace – of strangling her. And uh – She was then, I guess, just about six weeks -- but even at that age she *knew* and she just *froze*. Just like that. It was the most terrifying thing to see -- the fact that the husband had rejected her and rejected me has to play a big factor in it too. You become really animal, I think, over the whole process. The civilization drops away completely -- I have had absolutely no desire to have children at all. I don't even want to go near children. And I've never gotten over that" (G: 339, 342 CF.G: 182).

One couple's year old girl suffered from asthma and had been hospitalized several times with critical attacks. Doctors had told them that future children would probably also be asthmatic and that the disorder was likely but not certain clear up with adolescence. Says the mother, obviously under heavy strain: "if you have two children and they're both asthmatic – a mother could quietly go insane. Also, with two children, I just wouldn't be able to divide my time properly between the children. I would always be being unfair to one, if one were in the hospital. I had seen – when I had been in the hospital with our child – mothers who also had children home and could not be with their child in the hospital because of the responsibilities at home -- we could *not* take the chance of having *two* children going through this. It would just be unbearable I know I – I – my husband felt that I couldn't stand the strain. And I probably couldn't. Because I was so upset with –with her --but even if we had a *healthy* child somebody would have to suffer; you see? If our daughter were still in and out of the hospital, either the second child, or she would have had to suffer" (G: 318, 320, and 331). There is hardly a predicament in either book that inspires more sympathy than these two.

The situation is of a different cast when the man and woman are single and unlikely to marry. One man, thirty-one, a mechanic says: "she wanted to have the kid but it seemed totally unreasonable to me. There was no way I could handle any part of a kid right now. I have enough trouble keeping my own life in a straight direction without taking care of a kid. I just couldn't handle it. I didn't think it was good for her either. If I'd been in love with her, maybe I could have settled down, but it would have been the kid controlling our lives" (F: 125–26).

And as one young man put it to his pregnant girlfriend: "lookit, you're just sixteen and I'm four years older than you. So when you're eighteen you might just look around and say, "here I am, eighteen and my whole life's ahead of me and here I am stuck with a kid" (G: 199).

A twenty-one year old woman living with one man with her little boy by another, explains: "we both want a lot of things and with one child we can get it, but with two, I don't know, because I'm not working -- -we want to have one, we don't want to bring a child into the world that can't be taken care of the way it's supposed to be taken care of. I'd rather have an abortion than to make it suffer" (F: 56).

The problem of a divorced woman was somewhat more complex: "I was also afraid if I did some crazy thing by going and having an illegitimate child my husband would try to take my daughter away from me because he'd already tried once. He's very puritanical. He would've made fireworks out of it. So I had to protect my own child by not having this child" (she had had three abortions) (f: 53).

CHAPTER EIGHTEEN
A MATTER OF NECESSITY

These are the reasons that women and men presents as having led them to terminate their pregnancies. In reviewing them one notes several things. First, whichever of many reasons is put forward, behind it there is most often the dominating matter of an unsettled or, more often, estranged relationship between the women and either her parents or her partner. Often the "reasons" are not the reasons but the occasions for decision. Second, one would read through all of these stories in vain to find examples –particularly examples that might sustain some critical scrutiny and might be offered as illustrative of the need for abortion on demand –one would, I say, search in vain to find examples that are really compelling, that would justify the expression so frequently used: "we had to have the abortion."

In most of the stories both women and men are telling us that they simply did not wish to accept the burden or embarrassment the childbirth would have laid on them. (In most cases the issue is pregnancy and childbirth, not parenthood, because other willing and suitable families are willing to adopt the children.) Fasten your attention on the other cases, those where some sort of predicament is imposed from without only the woman or the couple and often you'll find that there was faint desire for the child anyway. There is a pervasive impression left with the reader that the reason why most children were not wanted is simply that they were not wanted.

Most of the interviewees were facing complications in their lives and frustrations and deprivations that were not of a magnitude beyond what ordinary mothers and fathers have found woven through the fabric of their at – times weary lives. Unless one is prepared to argue that all parenthood is a burden beyond what folks should be expected to bear, it is not easy to gather among these cases the wherewithal for any forceful or compelling statement on behalf of elective abortion, let alone subsidized abortion.

The most persuasive case would be that of a woman who has been victimized by the very people she should have been able to rely on; one who's energies and generosity are vouched for by a record of service wherein she has already extended herself so much that one could wonder whether she has not approached the limit; and one whose decision not to bear a child is endorsed by a consistent and responsible use of contraception. And this is the kind of women (with her husband or mate) who is so hard to find in these stories.

Most of the people who state that they cannot give more of themselves do not appear to have spent them selves much on others, quite apart from the matter of another birth. My point in making this observation is not to argue that these men and women are therefore obviously qualified to have children. They're obviously not. The arguments and explanations offered for these abortions are persuasive in this respect that they show the person's interviewed to be, by and large, not very desirable as parents.

This is a question all together distinct from their justifications for abortion. But the stories as told will not sustain a commonly held belief that abortion is resorted to by ordinary women who have been victimized innocently by friend or fortune and who must emerge from this untypical moment of trial by resorting to abortion. Folly is too much involved in these predicaments: much of it the folly of the abortors themselves.

CHAPTER NINETEEN
ADOPTION AS AN ALTERNATIVE

It is significant that very few reasons for abortion are offered by any of the persons interviewed. What reasons they do put forward are reasons not to have a child. They are, then, reasons either to contracept or to discontinue a sexual relationship that is untrue or unwise. In these books there is, it should be noted, scarcely any self – reproach for haphazard or desultory contraception and virtually none for untrue sex. Since so many of the speakers believe and assert that abortion is a much more drastic procedure than contraception or (possibly) sexual self discipline, that it imposes some physical hazard on a mother and extinguishes life in a way that raises serious moral concern, it would follow that to decide upon an abortion would require motives and reasons correspondingly more serious. Just the opposite is the case. The reasons that were insufficient to elicit either sexual self-discipline or responsible contraception are now invoked – with none new added – to explain the more chancy choice of abortion. Once again one stumbles into that incoherence, the puzzling absence of its all making sense.

One observes that there is no further set of reasons given for the choice to abort over other choices possibly less drastic. There is one significant exception, however. In the case of many women – especially those who are single or divorced - one option available would be to bear the child and offer too couples unable to bear children but willing and indeed anxious to share their homes and lives with sons and daughters. Traditionally this has been the course most recommended to pregnant, unmarried women, especially by those whose experience or observation dissuades them from recommending marriage in that circumstance. It is striking that adoption is so universally and heatedly discounted by the women in these interviews. They repudiate it has something they could not think of agreeing to.

Many of the young women indicate that adoption is simply not anything they had been prepared to think of as an option, like the teenager whose reaction to the suggestion (which she did later follow) was, "I was just so amazed. I had never considered that -- I never thought of people doing that" (G: 388).

Francke, in her essay on what single women face, hardly mentions adoption as a possible choice. Since day–care is so difficult to arrange and afford, "the social and financial pressure to terminate her pregnancy by abortion, therefore, becomes so great as to make it almost mandatory" (F: 45). Maxtone – Graham, herself adopted, is much more conscious of this as an option (as are the interviewees who were adopted) and her book offers much more frequent comment on adoption.

One finds ignorance, not simply of the possibility, but of the facts surrounding adoption. One woman, not a youngster but forty–four years old, thinks that "most babies that are "given away" are institutionalized" (G: 293). Another thinks that they are put in transient foster homes: "the abortion will be better than having the baby and then giving it up. I've been through foster homes myself, I couldn't do that to another person" (F: 90; CF. F: 142).

Even one mother who did choose adoption seems to believe that the outcome for her child is unlikely to be very reassuring. Alex was born and I saw him safely into what I felt was the best situation for him. Yes, he's going to have to deal with the mystery of "who are my parents?" (The counselor) and I talked about that long and heavy. But I think he stands a better chance of dealing and living with that mystery, if he's got parents, adoptive parents with him. And no matter how much he will scream at age thirteen, and no matter how many psychiatrists he may have to see, he still has the actuality of, "they wanted me, they came to get me, they kept me. I'm still here and tomorrow they'll still be there" (G: 182). Another who gave her child in adoption admitted, "Katrina, I don't feel good about it. I know that I did the right thing. I don't have to convince myself. There are just little moments of guilt" (G: 271).

What little familiarity and satisfaction with adoption is expressed comes entirely from women who have given children in adoption. One is emphatic about it. I could also give him safely into a home that wanted him. And I mean brackets (hitting table) positively, intellectually, emotionally the whole bit. "We want him, we know we want him. We have gone through the hell of the question of infertility, and through the adoption situation. We're clear – headed." And when this kid's spills his milk on the floor and your about ready to slap his head, "that's all right, kid, I wanted you." I don't want him to have a mother looking at him, no matter how much money she had, no matter how much society is changed, looking at him and thinking, "well, are you a mixed up leftover from a mixed up me "G: 181).

Another, more gentle, is also pleased with her decision: "also, if you're adopting a baby, you're much more likely to want the baby. Because you wouldn't go to all that effort to adopt her, otherwise. So, I felt she'd be far more secure. And thank God I didn't take her into that second marriage. That would have been unbelievably bad. You know, first with all of trouble she'd had in the early years and then to have a stepfather who was psychotic. And dangerous" (G: 349).

In the eyes of most of the women, though adoption is an abhorrent idea. "To have unmarried girls go through with it and then give it up for adoption; How – how can you be so cruel?" G.: 31).

And another: "no I don't approve of that! Not at all. I have very strong feelings about that. I think you have no right to do that to another human being. I don't think you have any right at all to create a human being and give it away. That is not your job in life. Just because it makes you feel a little better" (G: 292).

But apparently most of the women here would not feel better. Says one teenager, "one of the girls that he lives with -- had a baby last April. And the guy wouldn't marry her. He just told her to f--- off. And he went and enlisted in the army – in the Marines, for four years. So like she had the baby and her parents weaseled her into putting it up for adoption, you know? They really talked her into it; they brainwashed her.

And like, you know, she sees a little kid and she just – a little girl, about a year old and she looks at it – and she just flips out, you know? Because like it tore her apart, inside. And I

– I've had one nervous breakdown, when my dad split – he split three years ago – and I don't think, mentally, I could handle – you know, cope with giving away – and that girl, she just wishes that she'd kept her baby. But she couldn't have kept it because she really couldn't have given it the care that – you know, a baby needs. And so that's why she did it. And like abortions weren't legal then and otherwise she probably would have you know. It's really the easy way out" (G. 203–4).

Another woman, in her early twenties has similar misgivings: "you would wonder all your life, every little child, "I wonder if that's mine, "what would he or she be like now?" I don't believe I could ever have a child and give it up. I could have an abortion and forget that, much easier than I could have a child and give it up. Even if I never saw the child and even if they never told me whether it was a boy or girl. I would still always wonder. Oh, I wouldn't like to have that on my mind!"(G: 108).

Other women put a slightly different cast on the same worry. "I would never give up another child for adoption. Because I couldn't go through that again. And knowing I want the child so badly, if there was absolutely no way I could keep the baby, I would have an abortion -- I would think, "What am I doing? Giving away all my children? Will I ever have the chance to have my own?") G: 422 –23).

And a woman who had not had the experience says, "To me, the difficult thing would be to have a child and give it up. Like, I don't think I can do that. I think I would definitely want to keep my baby" (G: 53).

One of the comments labors under its own internal clash of ideas. At the suggestion of giving a child away instead of aborting it, the mother bridles: "oh my god! I couldn't even consider doing that! -- I mean I have absolutely no intention of giving it up! --I'm simply saying that I feel the child would be rightfully mine and that I would feel very cheated -- -- -- the choice to have the child is the choice to be a mother, it's not to give it up" -- -- --I really feel very strongly that mothers should not give up children, for their own sake. -- -- --after everything I've said it's going to sound very contradictory, but I – I'm not sure it is. I – I don't think it makes that much difference to the child. I think how the adoptive parents handle it is what makes a difference. -- I really don't feel giving up a child for adoption in terms of the child, is bad. I feel as a woman that it's absolutely unfair and ludicrous. I think at times there are real reasons for a woman not to keep a child but then she shouldn't have had it. She should have had an abortion!" (G: 84–86).

It is interesting to analyze the woman's understanding of "wanting a child." It seems a proprietary thing: to possess, to be satisfied with, to have. There is only a faint notion of joining one's life to another human being, of accommodating, being prepared to rearrange one's preferences for the sake of another. This Raggedy Ann attitude towards children emerges often in these stories.

But what of this vehemently negative view regarding adoption, this morale outrage that so many of the women express? The women who reject adoption as either hurtful to their offspring or hurtful to themselves reveal in their remarks this tendency to consider children as proprietary objects.

They are desired or annulled as the mother wishes, very much to suit her plans and needs. The mothers here may also be projecting onto adoptive parents their own instincts and commitments, neither which are very reliable

It is important to observe that this possessiveness, with less regard for the welfare of the child than for the dominant rights one may claim over him or her, is not characteristic only of young, unmarried women. There is another theme be found here and there throughout the stories: of fathers and of grandparents pushing themselves forward to block adoption and insisting that they "the family," keep the child. One teenager, facing her boyfriend's parents, was told by both of them that they opposed adoption of the forthcoming child because it would belong to them. She quotes the mother: "I do not believe in giving up babies for adoption." And she points to her son Kenny who's sitting there. "I never wanted him!" she says but I would never consider giving him up") G: 396–97).

There seems to be a general unawareness that adopted children are cared for by parents whose desire for them is, by and large, more demonstrably keen than that of physical parents. The interviewees would be uniformly astonished to discover that adopted children are emotionally and personally as well integrated as any – and sometimes a little more so.

This is all the more telling an item of ignorance in that the rejection of adoption brings many of these women and men most explicitly to the actual abortion decision. It differs from other "reasons" in that it would not serve also as a reason to contracept: it is a reason for aborting what has already been conceived. It is curious that this most salient factor in abortion choices should involve the most widespread misinformation. There is here considerably more ignorance about adoption than about contraception, to make but one comparison.

CHAPTER TWENTY
IS THERE A CHILD AT STAKE?

Whatever the components that combined to bring them to their choice, the women and men interviewed see abortion as a moral issue. This aspect is the subject of copious comment; even those who deny it as a morale problem take pains to say it so explicitly that they too end up entering their own ethical values into the debate. For instance, some say there is no child involved. One abortor recounts her conversation with her mother- in- law: "I told her my reasons and she said she could understand my reasons but she had always been taught and always believed that this was--well, I don't know, fratricide, [the killing of ones brother or sister] or whatever; that it was a life. And I said that I didn't consider it a life, that it was a mistake. And it wouldn't be a life until the baby was born and I just didn't want the baby to be born. So she – she's a nice woman and she understood my reasons – and she just said, "well I guess you've made up your mind" (G: 109).

Says a man about his girlfriend's abortion: "I went home and drank a couple of beers. I assumed everything was fine, so I didn't worry, I never thought about the baby at all. A baby's not a baby until it's born. And little babies don't do anything for me anyway. I never felt we were doing anything unhumane. It only made me feel guilty knowing she cared and I didn't. I felt guilty for not feeling more about it" (F: 126).

An eighteen-year old girl: "I didn't really think of it as a baby. I more or less thought of it as something that was going to be a baby, but not actually a baby. I didn't have any guilt feelings, like I was killing something" (F: 205).

And a seventeen year old "there's no way I wanted the baby. But I didn't think of it as a baby. I just didn't want to think about it that way" (F: 201).

There are repeated hints that one's moral judgment on abortion is correlated to what one finds comfortable. Some women are explicit about this and state that it is their outlook which, simply by being theirs, is decisive of the issue. "I really don't have any strong feelings that when a woman is first pregnant that there's any kind of reality about a "human being" inside of her. I think that she makes it real if she so chooses. I mean I see pregnancy very much as a purely physical state, that's not unrelated to any other physical state. Growing something inside of you – it's no different than a plant, you know. And I really feel that the thing that makes it real is the choice to have the child. And the choice to have the child is the choice to be a mother; it's not to give it up." I mean, this is terribly real to me" (G: 85).

This woman has had the experience of three abortions. Another, who has had two in her early twenties, recounts: "I never felt anything about the fetus. Before the abortion, I'd had one or two thoughts about it, but in my agony I only thought about myself. It's much easier not to think about the fetus, after all. The world will be a lot better place if there were fewer babies in it. That's the important thing" (F: 158).

Another, now married, says: "to me, it was absolutely a collision between a sperm and an egg and I don't feel at all that I did away with a human being. Nor does he. The point was that I was able to make a decision as an independent person. I had control over my own life and body. And I think that's really important" (G: 125).

Here again, the woman's negative feelings are not unrelated to her determination that the fetus has no human status. When those feelings are explicitly hostile, the moral issue is the more firmly prejudged. "I never thought about the fetus. I had a pre – political feeling of what was inside me and my rights. It was something that didn't belong there and had no place in my life at that time. I'd hated it before the abortion, but mostly I hated the man" (F: 50).

And an older woman recalls: "I went to planned parenthood. I went on my own and had a suction abortion. It sounded exactly like my vacuum cleaner. It was ghastly and graphic, like the hose had something caught in it. I should have put cotton in my ears. But I had no feeling about the baby. I didn't think of it as a baby. I had no emotional attachment to it. Hell, you can make one of those things every month. Once it's born I wouldn't give it up. But a fetus is unique only in the statistical sense" (F: 105).

As far as the baby was concerned, it was like before. I had gotten rid of something that hurt. It was not that I'd gotten rid of a living creature. I didn't feel it before and I guess that's why I didn't feel it afterward" (F: 102).

"To me it was a simple medical procedure and that's all. It was just more complicated in terms of appointment and traveling and getting there and coming up with the money and subterfuge – which my husband resented more than I

-- it was not a question of morality. We had no question of this is immoral, or we were killing a fetus, or any of this mythology" (G: 229,232).

No one among the nearly 100 persons interviewed addresses the morality of abortion as a serious intellectual issue, or offers a moral defense of having chosen it on grounds other than her or his own feelings. Feelings are invariably the determinant factor, not principles or evidence or facts are even ideas. The woman last quoted evidently considers the contrary position is not intellectually serious. Another states that she has in fact looked at the matter objectively:

"so I -- on a purely intellectual level, I didn't want the child, didn't want to have it. Didn't want to keep it. And there was no question of keeping it. I mean it was a decision that had been much mulled over and discussed, before the actual question arose. And when it did arise, I realized I still felt the same way. That even though you don't want to do this thing to yourself, you – you don't change your mind on a purely emotional basis. That's because you are pregnant, "you must therefore keep the child because it's a life." I don't think I really saw it as a life in the sense that I was, you know, sort of committing a murder. I certainly did not see it that way. At all" (G: 36).

What the woman has considered intellectually are her reasons for not wanting a child; the issue whether she has taken life or not she deals with, despite her disclaimer, in terms of what she wishes.

One youngster, after an abortion at the sixth week, remembers, "I just saw a pan full of blood with this little blob in it; that's all, that's all it was. But when it's inside of you, it's a – it's so different – you know? It really is. But when you see it floating around in blood, it's different" (G. 198; cf. G: 212).

A much older woman portrays a similar feeling, but pursues it further: "I never thought about the baby. Having had all those miscarriages and flushed so many fetuses down the toilet, it's not a baby to me. If it's just a medical procedure. But then I was only eight weeks pregnant. I could never abort a fetus that moved" (F: 109).

The moral attitude, grounded as it is in the complex emotional welcome, the woman has or does not have for a child, is affected by whether the fetus stirs within her in a recognizable human way. Francke observes that "many studies point out that first- trimester (abortors) discuss their abortion experience in terms of" the "pregnancy" or "the fetus". Late (abortors on the other hand, use such terms as "the "baby" or "the child" and refer to the procedure as "labor," "delivery" and "childbirth." Instead of expressing their feelings afterwards as slight grief or loss the late group often uses the term "mourning" (F: 83).

This finding is contradicted throughout these stories, where women and men persistently speak of "baby" and "child" (as does Francke herself) and rarely about "fetus," regardless of when the abortions take place. What is applicable in the finding is a reminder that pregnancy summons up some of the most powerful and dominating emotional forces. When those reactions put on a face that is hostile or unwelcoming they seem to block out any intellectual deliberation on the morality of abortion and to assign the unborn a moral importance proportionate to whatever readiness there is to accept him or her at birth.

CHAPTER TWENTY ONE
INCOHERENT REASONS, INCOHERENT MISGIVINGS

One would assume that from an interview sample of persons who had made choices – sometimes repeatedly – for abortion, there would be more moral comment in favor of abortion than on the other side. Curiously, the women and men in Francke's and Maxtone–Graham's books register as many misgivings as affirmations about what they have chosen to do. For some it is not an analytical judgment but a persistent sense of loss or wrong. "I sort of forgot the abortion afterwards, but I always felt guilty" (F: 77). "I felt terrible after the abortion. Sean had asked me to call him and I did. He was reserved but relieved that I was all right. I had a tough time at the ballet.

The last dance was a circus scene in which there were a lot of children dancing around. One was a little girl around seven or eight who had strawberry blonde hair, pigtails and freckles. I shed a few tears in the dark and thought, I just killed my own child. I've always wanted a girl and she looked just like me. It made me feel really bad. I felt really bad lying on the table right after the abortion too. I felt horribly sad at what I'd done and started to cry. My doctor held my hand and said I'd feel better about it soon. He assured me I could have another child when it was the right time for me" (F: 167–68).

Others are more direct and explicit. One woman retells the confrontation between herself and her parents: "he said he did not consider it a grandchild; he never would. My mother said she did not consider it a living thing. And this completely flipped me out. I mean, while she's saying this I can feel the baby moving inside of me. And I kept thinking, "How can she say that? She's been pregnant; and she knows what it's like to feel the life inside of her." I just couldn't understand how she – a woman – could say something like that" (G: 393).

Karen, a professional woman who has had three abortions, recalls: "I hated myself. I felt abandoned and lost. There was no one's shoulder to cry on and I wanted to cry like hell. And I felt guilty about killing something. I couldn't get it out of my head that I'd just killed a baby" (F: 61).

Or, as another woman remembers, "he assured me we could have another baby someday. I want a daughter. All I thought about is that this is a daughter. I want one so bad. I feel so sad. I feel like my daughter just went down the tubes. I feel like I abandon her. Oh, I feel so bad. I'd never do this again" (F: 96–97).

And another: "my feeling at that time was not one of shame, but of sadness. I tried not to think of the fetus as a baby, but I did. I wanted it over as quickly as possible emotionally. Mostly I wanted the option of divorcing my husband. That was the prime reason for the abortion" (F: 107).

Some of the interviews present an even more direct judgment on abortion. To the extent that it is admitted to destroying offspring, it stands in need of justification. The position of a twenty two year old who suffered a hysterectomy in the wake of her abortion is best caught by reproducing a segment of her interview

Katrina: what would you say on the "murdering" issue? As far as you yourself are concerned, do you feel you committed a murder?

Sandy: yes. Yes, I do. It's a human being. I really do. I think it's a very technical question: which human being is more valuable or has a greater right to live. But that baby, or that young fetus, or whatever it was, was having a tremendous effect on my body. I mean, there it was, growing.

Katrina: so would a cancerous growth.

Sandy: yes but this was not a cancerous growth. This had all the genes and all the potential of being like us. Not just "potential," it was going to be. I can't buy the theory that at a certain point that unborn becomes human.

Katrina: could you have, maybe, "killed in self defense"?

Sandy: yes, I feel that way. (G: 150 – 51)

Previously in her interview, Sandy had explained: "I really considered abortion wrong. And I still do. I have never said to myself that abortion is the right thing to do. I think now my attitude is that abortion, in my case, saved my life as my life is. It left me so that I could still communicate with my family. I can still have a job. It didn't totally destroy everything I was. And it was sort of a choice between me and that baby" (G: 132).

Another woman tells her mother in law, who had tried to talk her out of abortion because she would be taking a life, "I just feel that my life is more important to me right now."

A woman facing her third abortion states:

I'd like to get married and have a baby, but I doubt I ever will. I look too much for love and adoration and I get them mixed up with sex. I guess I do it to get people to validate me. If someone frowns, I always think it's because they're mad at me. I never think about the babies at all. But I fantasize when I'm around little kids. I pretend their mine. I live vicariously off of other people's children. I have regrets and that's when they come in. I want. But I keep denying it. Every time I talk about it, though, I want to pound the walls and scream and beat the carpets. I remember a conversation I had with a friend who'd just had an abortion. It's just an embryo, I told her, preferring to use the clinical definition. It's not a being, just a bunch of splitting cells. My friend said its murder. How can you deny it's a life" It's murder, but it's justifiable homicide. Now if I took that as my own philosophy I couldn't follow through with it. I'd have to have the baby. I agree with her, of course, but I just won't admit it. We've gotten very distant now. Maybe I should go to a psychiatrist, but I really don't have the money or the interest. Truth is hard to take and I'd just don't know if I'm ready for it. (F: 63).

Some of the women are less assertive and express only a resigned sort of low – level misery about abortion. "I lay on my back with my knees up. I knew inside it was all wrong, but all I could think about was what else could I do" (F.73–74).

Another: "I was very much against abortion at the time. I thought I was killing a living thing. And it didn't help much to overhear them talking in the hospital when I had it, saying, "Oh, it's a baby boy." I was almost seven months pregnant and I was born myself two months early that got to me more than anything" (F: 84).

A last kind of negative feeling about abortion comes in garbled form. A professional man reflects on his experience with a former companion: "ideologically we were both for abortion. But in our own case, there is a great deal of an ambiguity. There was the reality of this little person who was mine and hers who probably would have been a good kid. Late at night I thought about killing my own little son or daughter, but I also knew that it was a problem that had to be corrected -- -- --in a different world, abortion would be wrong. In this world, it's a necessity of evil. There are too many people, too many f---- up people. But that's just a rationalization. It could happen again. But it's nothing I could ever feel good about. And that surprised me. With men, I think, there's confusion between potency and virility. At least I feel more manly for having made a baby. But I still have the residual feeling of having killed something, a life that was already in impinging on mine. I've never resolved it" (F: 139–41).

Another view, more bewildering than bewildered, it is offered by the mother of an abortor. Francke introduces her: "Jessica Kroner, fifty-one, is a vibrantly attractive woman who, after twenty-five years of marriage, divorced her husband and entered the social and political chaos of the sixties with the same energy as her then teenage children. More of a friend to the children then the traditional mother, Jessica insists they call her by her first name.

When her daughter, Karen, had her first abortion at fifteen, Jessica was very supportive and indeed pleased to be able to help her. Jessica was equally pleased, when Karen had another abortion last year, that she was mature enough to handle it on her own and tell her only after the fact. Jessica lives in Philadelphia where she is active in politics" (F: 220).

And this is what Jessica says: "when she had the first abortion, she said to me, "I recognize it as murder and I'm willing to do it." Boy, was I impressed with that. Really impressed. I hope she won't do it to herself again. But she's still so desperately vulnerable to being hugged. I try to hug her all the time, but I guess it's not enough" (F: 222).

And a young girl named Betsy offers similarly thwarted reflections: "once I got the arrangements made, I really looked in the mirror and tried to imagine that there was a child there. I just, with every stretch my imagination, tried to make myself believe. And I – I do believe there was a child in there.

And I, you know, I'm sorry! I didn't want to -- -- -- to kill it. And I think I did. But I – I also – you know, I can't honestly say I regret it at all. You know when you're confronted with a situation like that (she was twenty one, living with eleven other students, including her boyfriend, in an apartment on a special work study project), you can't – you can't wish for a possibility that isn't there. That is, that I had never, you know, become pregnant" (G: 54).

Once again, there is the incoherence one has noticed throughout these stories. Misgivings about abortion are grounded on the same emotionality that is used to justify it. In the end, it is still the mother that is the measure of the child's worth. Even when, in starkest terms, it is said that one has taken her own child's life, that judgment is estopped: it does not carry across with the urgency or force the moral judgments commonly have. It's canceled out by a statement either that the child is not desired or that its life should go forfeit for that of the mother. When these two lives are weighed in the balance, what is meant by "life" has equivocal meaning. There is never any consideration that the harm to which the woman is liable is of an entirely different kind and magnitude than the harm facing the offspring. The claims of the mother override both consideration and granting of that.

Franck observes, "a common phrase many women use in describing their dilemma is" I want an abortion even though I know it's murder." To Martha Mueller, a counselor at a Planned Parenthood clinic in Brooklyn, that phrase is a definite sign of ambivalence" (F: 32).

It may signify a something more than ambivalence. There is a clean contradiction here and an unresolved one. The moral issue, so strenuously debated by those at some distance, is dealt with by those closely involved in so incoherent a way that one is pressed to inquire further how this can be so.

CHAPTER TWENTY TWO
RELUCTANCE ABOUT MORAL JUDGMENT

The youngest women and men stumble about these pages with a stunted sort of moral sense. Missy, fifteen, says: "I kept thinking about what it would be like. I want a boy. My boyfriend and I named him mark -- -- --I don't want to ever have another abortion. It's a very frightening thing. The injection hurt a lot. But mostly I thought about the baby when they were doing it. I thought, I'm killing another human being, but then I'd remember that it wasn't even formed yet. I had two sides going in my mind against each other. But I'm glad for the most part I had the abortion" (F: 199–200).

June, eighteen: "another thing that makes me feel guilty is my cousin. She had two abortions and I talked to her Friday and she said my other cousin had a book showing how the baby looked and she said if I was to see the pictures I'd really be upset about it. I think it's just best for me because I can't afford another kid right now" (F: 203).

Molly, sixteen: "the abortion sort of bothers me, too. My friend says it's not a baby yet. It's not a baby until after fifteen weeks; then is starts to develop into a baby. She said it's just like tissue right now. It makes me feel a little better about it, but still -- -- -- it does bother me. And I can't talk to my mother about this sort of thing. We're catholic and my dad especially is a strict catholic. Abortion is just out of the question. I went to a parochial school till eighth grade, so I was taught that it's wrong to destroy a life. Every life has a right to live. So I have that on my mind too, but it's my decision. I couldn't take care of a baby right now, I don't think" (F: 188).

Yet there is an incoherence here that survives youth. Virginia, seventy-three, says) of her abortion fifty years previously): "when I finally came to, I asked what it was. They said it was an 8 1/2 pound boy. It was a beautiful fetus, they said, which made me feel better -- he would have had a miserable life. And besides, though his father was a very sensitive lover, he was ugly" (F: 238).

It is difficult to evaluate this chiaroscuro [the arrangement of light and dark] of moral judgment. In many of the cases the participants glimpse something unpleasant in the abortion and glance away from it. In others there is an uncanny ability to gaze into the face of chaos and not be confounded.

Two men exemplify this. One now separated from his girlfriend. (Unmarried abortors tend to separate from their impregnated partners in these stories and many of the married also go their separate ways), remembers: "there was some kind of tug at the thought of the baby. It was not a fatherly one, but one of unease. We both cracked tasteless jokes about it months later, like how they disposed of it or whether it could have survived in salt water. Neither of us wanted to confront that we had wiped out something alive.

So we played games. It's just like war when you end up calling the enemy gooks" (F: 137).

Another man, a black musician, married has this memory: "the loss of the baby didn't bother me at all. I didn't think about it. I was more concerned with her welfare rather than having a child at that time. If anything, it was like the child was not there, that we were not going to have a kid; that she was having an operation just to get cooled out. She could have been having her appendix out and it wouldn't have made any difference to me at that time. I must have blocked it out, because of course it did matter" (F: 176).

Catherine, forty four, looks back to an abortion when she was half that age. At first she seems to equivocate, then seems to adopt an ethical stand. One is left uncertain, however, whether she is clearer when she is unsure or when she is sure:

Well, many women have more than one abortion. Many women. And if they had enormous emotional hang-ups, if their grief over this particular, quote, "child" was such, they wouldn't do it the second time -- -- -- and it's pretty apparent that this is a very ambivalent kind of thing; in other words, "this is a child, but it's not a child." - -- --generally, with catholic girls who are troubled by the concept that they have "a baby and that they are now going to murder" and, of course, a fair percent of the of the problem ladies have with abortion would be eliminated tomorrow, if we would all stop referring to this as a "baby" – where we conjure up this little thing that you're holding in your arms with its blue eyes and its little face. – this is not what you're dealing with, when you're talking about an eight week pregnancy -- -- as you probably notice, I am a highly rational human being -- -- also societies, when they are desperate to control the population, reach out to the most extreme methods they can find – including infanticide.

Most people don't realize that, but it's true. when you must control your population and you don't know how to do it, what do you do? You kill the babies that are born. That's the only logical thing to do. Americans look at me with his look on their faces as if I have just, you know, who said the most hideous thing in a world – because I'm prepared to realize that people murder other human beings, which they must do. (G: 301-2, 309, 313, 314)

One notices a frequent distinction between early and late abortions, from an ethical perspective. Many women who see no moral problem in first–trimester abortions would draw the line at those in the second trimester, after they can feel their child moving (some would "draw the line" by refraining from this kind of abortion; the stories suggest that many would go ahead anyway but feel more disturbed later). Says one abortor: "I really couldn't think of it as being you know, murder, to me. Because I had an abortion before I was quite six weeks pregnant. I had no feeling for the child. I could never have waited until the fourth month or so when the child was kicking. I would have started to have feelings for the child, when the child started to act" (G: 327).

Second trimester abortions (and, for that matter, third – trimester ones, which are legal and do occur, but are not much mentioned in these interviews) are difficult even for the medical staff, according to Francke's account.

Joyce Craigg, director of a Brooklyn clinic of Planned Parenthood, worked in surgery assisting in late abortions for two months, then quit "the doctors would remove the fetus while performing hysterotomies and then lay it on the table, where it would squirm until it died. One catholic doctor would call for sterile water every time he performed a hysterotomy and baptize them then and there.

They all had perfect forms and shapes. I couldn't take it. No nurse could" -- -- -- women undergoing second – trimester abortions have cause to be disturbed. In many hospitals, for example, the fetus is expelled (the medical jargon is "slipped") and left lying on the bed until the afterbirth is also expelled.

There is a natural curiosity for the women to look at the fetus a curiosity the nurses try to squelch. "We tried to avoid the women seeing them," says Norma Eidelman, who worked for a short time with second trimester patients. "They always wanted to know the sex, but we lied and said it was too early to tell. It was better for the woman to think of the fetus as an "it." Then we'd scoop up the fetuses and put them in a bucket of formaldehyde, just like Kentucky Fried Chicken. I couldn't take it any longer and I quit."(F: 33 – 34)

The consistent repugnance for late abortions discloses the understructure of all moral statements, pro and con, made by the women and men who speak in Francke's and Maxtone – Graham's books. There is an intensified emotional awareness of one's unborn offspring, Because of quickening: the heartbeat is heard about the tenth week, movement is felt in these months and the swelling begins to be apparent.

Also, the procedures for abortion after the first trimester are more palpably violent: the fetus is either poisoned and then delivered dead; or delivered early by inducing or by caesarean section and then left to die; or dismembered alive in the womb and evacuated in pieces. Both factors can have a powerful impact on the women and the attendants.

What is at stake here, however, is not a more advanced fetal development which allows them now to acknowledge that it is indeed a human being (that notion is present throughout but suppressed); it is a more poignant emotional annunciation by the fetus that challenges the emotional denial turned towards it.

The distinction between first trimester and later abortions is more one of instinct and emotion than of the mind none the persons expressing distaste for the latter procedure sees the palpable, visible development of the fetus at this advanced stage as evidence of what has been unfolding and present all along.

Quickening is not taken as verification or even a suggestion that, on principle, womb–life is a continuum. Nurses who revolt at hysterectomies and salting–out and prostaglandin [substance derived from fatty acids] abortions simply restrict themselves to vacuum procedures rather than questioning what might be common to all techniques.

What is at stake is not the status of the being in gestation, but whether it has broadcast to the woman bearing it or to the persons aborting it enough of an emotional appeal for her or for them to *feel* it as a child. It is as in the many stories that told how the unborn had to be wanted before being accredited as a child. The mother is still the measure of the offspring.

The status of humanhood is conferred and the ethical issue resolved, not by acknowledging the unborn as human, but by deciding whether those who hold the power of life and death wish to confer this status and protection. The visa to life is a grace, not a right.

CHAPTER TWENTY THREE
WHO ARE THE ABORTORS

What are the situations of the women who speak here? Do they justify the public presentations made on their behalf? "But I am only twelve years old." No twelve year olds or subteens among them.

"I was raped." No rape victims, though one woman was set upon by a priapic [preoccupied with sex] and sodden husband one night.

"We'll have to go on relief." No one here is quite in this situation.

"My father will kill me." All the teenagers say this; although in some instances one might cheer the father on, it is not a serious fear.

"The doctor says it will die before it's two." No doctor says that here.

"My IUD failed." Once here. "I'm 50; I thought I couldn't get pregnant." No fifty year olds here; only one who is in her forties; a dozen plus in their thirties; the typical age is the early twenties.

There are certainly women in the land who come to abortion in the circumstances described by the NARAL advertisement with which this essay began, but they are very few. And they are not the clientele for whom abortion is provided. The clientele in these pages, more representative, is a group of women relatively unsettled with their men, pushed a bit by pressures and bold in the company of those who will not say them nay.

They have not yet sorted out well the give–and–take of life shared and they choose now to take more and share less. Their abortions have not wrecked their lives. They have not resolved them. The same disorder, the same incoherence, seems to continue. The abortions do not deal with the problems investing their lives and, in fact, may even distract them from these problems.

One of the women sums it up: "Abortion, be it legal or illegal, paid for or not, is here to stay. It is not up to men to tell women what to do under these circumstances. Nor is it up to women to tell each other what to do. Solving the dilemma of an unwanted pregnancy is probably the single most important decision an individual will ever have to make. And regardless of whether she chooses to continue her pregnancy or to terminate it through abortion, it is her decision alone. So it falls to all of us to support that decision with grace, safety and understanding–and to live with it and each other, as best we can" (F: 257).

Those are Linda Bird Francke's closing words. What she describes as the ambivalence of abortion, however, is not really ambivalence it is incoherence: the crazy incoherence that comes when one tries to walk through a contradiction. Like declaring a nation based on rights to life, liberty and the pursuit of happiness, guaranteed to all and at the same time denying these rights to slaves.

That is not ambivalence. Like providing equal protection under the law for all citizens and denying the vote, the jury and the bar to women. That is not ambivelance. Like saying that it is one's child one carries in the womb and disposing of it and will. That is not ambivalence. These are contradictions and experience shows that we are capable of living incoherently, putting off justice, for a long time indeed.

The testimony of those women and men who recount their personal experiences of abortion compels a strong human sympathy. The last thing in the world it does is to sustain an acceptance of abortion. It tells, story after story, the tale of how unborn young lives have been the wastage of an incoherence, disaffiliation and self–indulgence and repugnance for truth that afflicts their parents. Here is testimony to a most a dismal, even an uncannily spiritual, extinguishing of fertility, of life planted and unable to grow from withered stock.

One final word. The movement for women's rights is composed of many strands and fibers of issue and interest. I expect that they will be unraveled and braided again into new combinations in years to come. At this time those who see abortion as a tragedy tend to hold themselves at some distance from the woman's movement because some of its vocal leaders are partisans for abortion choice. This might be otherwise

Anyone who understands abortion as part of a complex convulsion within family should be mighty and vigorous in defense of the equality for women. There will always be some abortion, as Francke says; there will always be infanticide and parricide [murder of father and mother] and rape. But the colossal number of abortions sought now in our country seems in some respects to be epidemic. It is not due simply to the contemporary hostility towards children, nor to a resolute campaign of public persuasion, nor to the recent legalization, nor even to the irresponsible use of contraception. It is due in some measure to the fact that age–old patterns in the family have been abruptly repudiated it.

Women are chafing under denials of appreciation, opportunity and freedom that hurt much more now, after the inadequacy has been drawn to our attention but before it has been remedied. Men, who for all that time as unwitting as women in perpetuating the inequities, came in for hostile treatment they do not want to accept as merited. It little matters; there must be a change. It will require clout, for advantage is rarely given up without a push. But much more than clout, it will require great wisdom.

Equality is not that hard to come by; it is equality in family that is the problem. The family needs to be renegotiated: not in the clumsy, life depriving ways described in these stories, but in ways that will produce fewer sullen and selfish women or impotent men. When that comes, many then will be too wise and too committed to choose abortion.

NOTES

(ESSAY 1 RACHEL WEEPING: THE VETERANS OF ABORTION) P. 1-35, 59, 60

1.   See, for comparisons, Zimmerman's study of 40 mostly young abortors, which is largely congruent with the materials analyzed here: Mary K. Zimmerman, *Passage through Abortion*: The Personal and Social Reality of Women's Experiences (New York: Praeger, 1977) See also Judith G. Smetana, "Beliefs about the Permissibility of Abortion and Their Relationship to Decisions regarding abortion," Journal of Population 2, no 1 (Spring 1979), 294-305.

2.   "Contrary to the popular belief that shame over pregnancy out of wedlock is the major motivation for abortion, we observed that.....much more importance was the woman's rejecting of motherhood with all is attendant demands. Our impression is that these women tend to be narcissistic and regard the fetus as a competitor for the succorance and dependent care they themselves obviously require." Charles Ford, Pietro Castelnuovo-Tedescoand Kahila D. Long, "Women Who Seek Therapeutic Abortion: A Comparison with Women Who Complete Their Pregnancies, "American Journal of Psychiatry 129, no 5 (November 1972) 551.

3.   Barbara Grizzuti Harrison, "On Reclaiming Moral Perspective," Ms., June 1978, p. 97.

CHAPTER TWENTY FOUR
A FUNDAMENTAL RIGHT*

Our most fundamental right is the right to life. The right to life is the right to all other rights. The dead don't have any rights.

What do the experts say? (The following as gleaned from http://www.prolife.org:80/ultimate/upl39.html)

I 1981 (April 23-24) a Senate Judiciary Subcommittee held hearings on the very question before us here: When does human life begin? To speak on behalf of the scientific community there appeared a group of internationally-known geneticists and biologists who had the same story to tell, namely that human life begins at conception. They told their story with a profound absence of opposing testimony. In other words their testimony based on fact and scientific research would be almost impossible to refute.

Dr. Micheline M. Mathews-Roth, Harvard Medical School, gave confirming testimony, supported by references from over 20 embryology and other medical textbooks that human life begins at conception.

"Father of Modern Genetics" Dr. Jerome Lejune told lawmakers: "To accept the fact that after fertilization has taken place a new human has come into being is no longer a matter of taste or opinion….it is plain experimental evidence."

Dr, Hymie Gordon, Chairman, Department of Genetics at the Mayo Clinic, added: "By all the criteria of modern molecular biology, life is present from the moment of conception."

Dr, McCarthy de Mere, medical doctor and law professor, University of Tennessee, testified: "The exact moment of the beginning of personhood and of the human body is at the moment of conception."

Dr. Alfred Bongiovanni, University of Pennsylvania School of Medicine, concluded, "I am no more prepared to say that these early stages represent an incomplete human being than I would be to say that the child prior to the dramatic effects of puberty….is not a human being."

Dr. Richard V. Jaynes: "To say that the beginning of human life cannot be determined scientifically is utterly ridiculous."

Dr. Landrum Shettles, sometime called the "Father of in Vitro Fertilization" notes, "Conception confers life and makes that life one of a kind. And on the Supreme Court ruling _Roe v. Wade_, "To deny a truth (About when life begins) should not be made a basis for legalizing abortion.

Professor Eugene Diamond: "…. either the justices were fed backwoods biology or they were pretending ignorance about a scientific certainty."

"Bet you never knew this" Department.

ROE V WADE
WRITING THE FINAL CHAPTER

The infamous Roe v Wade decision happened all because, "Jane Roe" the victim of a rape (which she later admitted never happened), became pregnant and appealed to the Supreme Court for the right to abort her child. By the time that decision was handed down, Jane Roe had already given birth and the child was placed for adoption. Since that 1973 case, however, more then two million abortions have been performed annually. What began as sympathy for a "Victimized" woman has resulted in the deaths of millions and millions of unborn babies.

The Surgeon General of the United States, C. Everett Koop has so aptly said (and I might add, prophetically proclaimed), "For every Baby Doe in the 1980's... THERE WILL BE 10,000 GRANNY DOES IN THE 1990'S."

The country that is headed by a man or woman who, without shame, acknowledges the existence and laws of God, is a nation destined, though with many a trial, to prosper and lead the world.

THE AUTHOR'S PERSONAL LETTER
TO A FRIEND

(On the occasion of a casual comment: "There have been more people killed in the name of Christianity than for any other reason.")

Dear Lou:

I enjoyed our conversation this afternoon at the 'Club.' I pray you will not be offended by this little letter. I knew that what you had stated, "More people have been killed in the name of Christianity, (or Religion) than any other way in the world," was not quite accurate. I must admit, Lou that this is a very popular misconception and is spread about on a daily basis by many people. It seems that some just delight in blaming Christians (Religion) for everything and in particular for the death of other humans.

There is no doubt that there has been some misguided Christians (if they were 'Christians' at all) that have sought to murder other humans in the name of God or Christianity, but you see Lou that would be the same as me stealing in your name and then the world holding you responsible when in actual fact you would not even condone stealing by anyone. Because I steal in your name does not make you an accomplice.

So having said that, let me now bombard you with some 'Real' facts about the deaths of millions of people and the part that Christians played or did not play in the total numbers.

About 170 million people have been killed by other human beings in this century. And this is a conservative estimate. About 130 million of these have died because of ATHEISTIC IDEOLOGY - whether it was Hitler's racism that viewed the Jews as human bacteria or Mao's attempt to liquidate Christianity in the Great Proletarian Cultural Revolution. All these deaths occurred because man rejected God.

To bring about communism, it was necessary to kill approximately ten million people, and Lou, certainly not in the name of Christianity, as is often said 'more people have been killed in the name of Christ and (religion) than any other name.' You know, Lou we hear this so often that many people take it as gospel truth. It is the farthest statement from the truth than any other often repeated statement. You know that old saying, "Say something often enough and long enough and sooner or later thousands will believe it." This is what has happened to the blaming of Christ, Christianity and/or Religion for the death of millions of people. It is simply untrue as simple research would prove in an instant.

Have more people been killed in the name of Religion than in any other way? No Lou, a thousand times, NO. More people have been killed in the name of Atheism than in the name of Christianity, or Religion. Far more have been killed by Marxists or Communists than were ever killed in the name of Christianity or the name of Religion. The number killed by atheists totally dwarfs the number of those killed by professing Christians, or in the name of any Religion.

The Inquisition: This is, without a doubt, horrible and inexcusable, but in truth, if you will pardon the 'quip' Lou, the inquisition was like a tea party compared to the purges of Stalin. Stalin showed no mercy at all when, as is generally agreed, he had forty million (40,000,000) humans killed during HIS purge. It has been said that during his (Stalin's) attempt to liquidate the entire Christian church and Religion he murdered the forty million

Hitler, who hated God as much as Stalin did, was the epitome of a racist. He killed Jews, Gypsies (most of whom were professing Christians, or belonged to a Religious sect), Slavs, Poles and others he deemed racially inferior such as the elderly, cripples, or the mentally handicapped.

The first victims of the holocaust were 70,000 insane and incurable people. And ironically, Lou, at this point it was only the courageous voice of two Christian leaders who spoke openly and publicly against this atrocity. The holocaust began with euthanasia. By the time Hitler (an atheist) was through he had murdered 6 million Jews and between 9 and 10 million others. Lou, as I mentioned earlier, all these facts and figures can be proven by a little research at the local library.

Revolution and Mao: It is estimated that Mao alone killed more than seventy million (70,000,000) Chinese.

In the first ten years after Mao's takeover in 1948, 24.7 million were killed in purges, famines, deaths in slave labor camps. From 1959 to 1962 about 25 million were killed or were starved to death.

Finally, from 1969 to 1976 in the Great Cultural Revolution of China, an estimated 22 million were killed. Dr. Barrett calls this "History's most systematic attempt ever, by a single nation to eradicate and destroy Christianity and religion." Mao was responsible for killing about 72 million people in total.

Cambodia: It is estimated that out of a nation of approximately seven million people, between two and three million were killed. None in the name of Christianity or Christ.

So, my very good friend, let's add up the numbers: Mao killed about 72 million between 1948 and 1976. Add to this Stalin's number of 40 million, we have 112 million (112,000,000). Now we throw in Hitler's 15 million (not counting the deadly war he started) and we come up with 127 million humans killed and none in the name of Christ or Christianity, or Religion. If we were to add those dead, from the wars of this century, the number killed would easily jump to 170 million.

So, Lou, how many have really been killed in the name of Christianity or in the name of Religion? If one were to use the most exaggerated criteria and numbers, one could come up with no more than 17 million people killed by Christians or professing Christians, and all of these in ***twenty centuries (2000 years)*** of Christian history. Those killed in the name of the SECULAR state in just this past **100 years** is about ten times more than those killed in the name of Christ and/or Christianity, or Religion (170 million versus 17 million).

What about the unborn? Well Lou, I won't bore you any longer, although I do hope I have made some progress in killing (no pun intended) a myth that seems to run rampant in certain circles. First of all there are millions alive today who would have been killed in the womb if it were not for the stand that Christians have taken against abortion. World wide, the present number of abortions is estimated at approximately one hundred million (100,000,000) per year.

This means that approximately two billion humans have been killed by abortion in the past twenty years. Lou, should we add these to the others that have been killed in other than the name of religion (170 million)? If we do add them to the total then those killed **NOT** in the name of Christianity, or Religion would be approximately two billion, one hundred and seventy million.

No, Lou, not religion but the 'State' (see the countries I have listed earlier) has proven itself to be the greatest killer of all times. And the 'State' (again pick the country) has proven itself to be a killer of religious and non religious people, in the millions, as it has attempted to eradicate Christianity and other religious sects.

I sometimes wonder why people hate Christians. It has never made any sense to me, even before I became a Christian myself. It seems that Christians and Christianity have become an acceptable target for anyone and everyone at any time, without real reason, cause or justification.

There is another very large numbered religion that no one says anything about because of fear.

Yet this religion condones the beating of women, the beheading of their own members if one of them becomes a

Christian and the murder of Christians if they try to spread the gospel or convert their members. These same people seem to find it perfectly acceptable to convert Christians. Strange happenings, Lou but Christians are an easy target because they prefer peace to violence and if someone is not going to do you violence then you can do or say what you want to them without fear.

Well, my dear friend, that is my input. This is a much better way for me to express my views with proper researched statistics rather than sit and argue. I pray you will not be offended by my humble offering.

May I say at this point, Lou. That if we had not engaged in the killing of the unborn then we would have had sufficient citizens to replace the ones that have died. Instead we have found that to keep the population growing we need to 'import' citizens from other countries. If we did not have abortion, we probably would not have the need for such a large influx of citizens. Am I against immigrants, no I am not, Lou, my parents were immigrants.

God bless you.

Terence

*BIOGRAPHICAL NOTES: FATHER JAMES BURTCHAELL:

FATHER BURTCHAELL is a fifth-generation Oregonian who was taught by Holy Cross priests at their high school in Portland and decided to join them. This took him to his studies at Notre Dame, Rome, Washington, Jerusalem and Cambridge, where he earned his Ph.D. in theology. He was ordained a Holy Cross priest in 1960and began teaching theology at Notre Dame in 1966. During his years as a teacher there he held other responsibilities as department chairman and later provost and trustee of the University.

Since 1990 he has lived near Princeton and then in Phoenix at a residence of the Holy Cross fatherland devoted his time to research and writing.

This is what Father Burtchaell has to say about his professional work:

My theological work has been historical in mode, revisionist in manner and somewhat diverse in subject matter. I like to take a topic about which I have a hunch that the received understanding has somehow gone wrong and then study the evidence sustaining a different interpretation. My current research interest is the ways ethicists work and say they work. What I find fascinating about the subject is how we use our imagination to do our moral reasoning.

James T. Burtchaell's listings are extensive and impressive, giving those who read his work, the feeling that he can be trusted to have done the research necessary to produce an honest work of high quality and integrity. How one may wish to interpret what he has written will be the responsibility of each individual. Nonetheless…there can be no doubt that his arguments are compelling and worthy of a reader with an investigative mind who is seeking the truth.

LISTINGS:

Who's Who:
Who's Who in the Midwest
Who's Who in the East
Contemporary Authors
Who's Who in Religion
Directory of Systematic Theologians in North America
Leaders in Education
The Writer's Directory
International Who's Who
International Who's Who in Community Service
International Scholars Directory
American Catholic Who's Who
National Social Directory
Directory of American Scholars
CSSR (Council of Societies for the Study of Religion) Directory of faculty
Outstanding Writer's of the 20th Century

ABOUT THE AUTHOR

The author was born in Montreal March 12, 1940. Has traveled extensively and loves to write. He is currently working on his memoirs. He has lived in the wilderness for three years in a 15 foot trailer, was president of a Spear Fishing Club in the Bahamas and was one of the last persons to spend a vacation with Robert Kennedy, in the Bahamas, just prior to Mr. Kennedy's assassination. Of Mr. Kennedy, he says, "A kind, loving intellectual who always showed concern for those less fortunate."

Printed in the United States
51201LVS00001B/37-54